Affordable Homes in Rural Scotland

– the role of housing associations

RAYMOND YOUNG

and voices from rural associations

Memories of happy days in housing
Best wishes,
Donald x

Capercaillie Books

First published by Capercaillie Books Limited in 2015.

Registered Office Summit House, 4–5 Mitchell Street, Edinburgh EH6 7BD.

© Raymond Young

The moral rights of the author have been asserted.

A catalogue record of this book is available from the British Library

ISBN 978-1-909305-922

Printed by Bell & Bain Ltd, Glasgow

Contents

This book is dedicated to the many voluntary committee members of rural Housing Associations, without whom there would have been no story to tell, and without whom many people would still be living in a caravan, a very poor quality home or would have been forced to move out of the countryside.

Author's Introduction to Part One

This book was edited and written by a townie. I was born in a city (Newcastle), brought up in another one (Glasgow), and worked in urban housing and regeneration for most of my days. I love the buzz of cities – the mix of people and cultures, the anonymity that it offers as well as the opportunities for bringing people together, the music, theatre and other entertainments that enrich both mind and soul. I'm a townie, even although I now live in a small Perthshire village. So who am I to write a book about rural housing?

I also love the countryside. Like many Scots, my ancestors came from the Highlands and the Islands and from Ayrshire. They had rural jobs and in the great migration towards the cities at the turn of the nineteenth and twentieth centuries they came seeking a better life in the central belt of Scotland in Glasgow and its surrounding towns. In the Highlands and Islands life was incredibly hard. Working a small croft with poor quality land and fishing in difficult waters to support a large family (my Highland grandfather had thirteen siblings) can have been no fun. Indeed my great grandfather, from Knoydart, Neil MacInnes and his brother William appeared before Deer Forest Commission in 1894. William led the evidence (Neil was questioned in Gaelic with an interpreter) and he explained that he had ten sheep, was allowed four cows and for most of his life had carried the mails from Knoydart to Isleornsay in Skye, but now the mails went via Mallaig (and this was before the railway reached Mallaig). The crofts were so small that *they wouldn't maintain one man for a year . . . they go far and near and even abroad to earn money for the families they leave at home. It is not the crofts at Airor that maintain the family'*. And what they wanted was more land so that they could stay in Knoydart, but while the owner had promised to rent them more land, it appeared that the Factor was not cooperating. The issues of land, its management, and employment run through the rural housing story.

So the countryside is somewhere in my genes even although my knowledge of agriculture and fishing is limited to being able to tell my wheat from my barley, my Aberdeen Angus from my Belted Galloway, and my herring from my mackerel. I've visited relations on Skye from an early age, walked the hills around Glasgow, cycled the back roads, had more bed nights on Iona than anywhere else away from my own bed, spent hours on Clyde steamers and on CalMac, and from time to time climbed the odd Munro. I've even tried to ski on the slopes of Glencoe. And that's rural Scotland for most of us townies. We see rural Scotland through the visitor gaze, without really trying to understand what life must be like now for those who want to make their living from the sea, the countryside or from a large number of non-agricultural activities and without whom we would not be able to enjoy one of the most beautiful and best bits on God's earth. We treat rural Scotland like a vast theme park, a pleasuredome, full of exotica from which we retreat back to our townie life. And we like it that way. We get up in arms when someone wants to develop and change that countryside. We want rural Scotland to stay like that. We often do not recognise the variety of employment and opportunities that there are outside our urban existence. But rural Scotland is not just a visitors' paradise. Tourism may now be its biggest industry, but agriculture, aquaculture and arboriculture still have a bright future, along with energy supply and other larger scale industries, while SMEs, the arts and education are thriving. And all of these need support services from posties to procurator fiscals, from nurses to neurosurgeons, from mechanics to masons. And all this means that people need somewhere to live.

Housing is at the heart of the future of rural Scotland. To most townies,

My great grandfather's house in Knoydart in 2013.

as we drive around the countryside, we think that people must have the best place to live because we don't see concentrations of slums while houses look neat and tidy. Could there be a rural housing problem? Is affordability an issue? And who is providing new homes?

I was tempted to give a very similar title to this book as a Rural Forum report from 1984 – 'Scotland's *Rural Housing – A Forgotten Problem*'. At the time of writing that was published just over thirty years ago. Much has happened since then to improve the situation and this book charts some of the successes. But challenges are still there – young people are still being forced to move because there is not sufficient housing. If you are rich you can buy land. If you have a low income, the choices are very limited – indeed there is a question of whether rural Scotland is being rapidly gentrified in the twenty-first century. Some of the conditions under which people are living are the poorest in Scotland, with very high levels of fuel poverty. But the difference today from the time when my great grandfather appeared before the Crofter Commission is that there is more work – rural Scotland now offers opportunities unimaginable to Neil MacInnes. It's a growing and dynamic part of Scotland, and people want to work and live there.

So why am I writing this? Twenty-five years ago I was given the opportunity and privilege of leading the team developing a rural housing policy for the then national housing agency – Scottish Homes. It was a fascinating period of working and learning with an amazing group of people across rural Scotland. My interest has continued through my involvement with Rural Housing Scotland, including ten years as its convener.

And while there have many accounts of one of the most exciting developments in rural Scotland within that twenty-five year period – that of the Community Buy Outs that feature whole communities such as Assynt, Eigg, and Gigha – there is little public appreciation of the pioneering work of housing associations which have helped transform the lives of many people and rural communities over the last thirty years. Their stories deserve to be told. Perhaps some of the family gene that led to that Crofter Commission appearance has come down through the generations and since no-one else has written the story Mary Taylor, the Chief Executive of the Scottish Federation of Housing Associations, cajoled me into writing it. I agreed on the basis that we should have a number of housing association voices in it. So the book is in three parts – first an overview for which I take full responsibility. Secondly, a collection of writings by a number of housing committee members and staff (both current and retired) who have voluntarily contributed their stories and I am very grateful to them. These stories provide a rich viewpoint, a grass roots counterbalance to the overview that comes from working at national policy level. I asked for volunteers at the Rural and Island Housing Association Forum conference in 2014 to write their story and most of those who volunteered have been published. Information from others has been incorporated into the overview. Inevitably there could have been many more stories but just as land is a controlling factor for housing, so is space in this book. I have tried to include both geographical and organisational variety – as well as a mixture of staff and volunteers. Perhaps this book might stimulate a web based library of stories . . .

The book comes with a health warning – this is not just an historical account. None of us involved comes from a totally objective or academic viewpoint. There are many more equipped to do a more objective assessment – I particularly commend 'The Rural Housing Question' by Madhu Satsangi, Nick Gallent and Mark Bevan as the latest serious but readable analysis. This book is aimed at those concerned about rural issues, about Scotland's rural past and future and in particular about rural housing to ensure that we remember where the rural housing association contribution has come from. It's a 'roots' type book. But I've also asked myself the question – what would one want to say if there was a Royal Commission today? And so the book ends with a third part setting out some reflections on where we are today and about the future. It may be useful to someone when we come to the election of the next Scottish Parliament . . . !

In writing this book I want to record my thanks to Mary Taylor for asking me to write and to pull together the book; to Diane Cooper at the SFHA who has patiently helped with photographs and the arrangements with Kay Strang of Capercaille Books; to my wife Jean for putting up with yet more time spent with the computer; to Derek Logie of Rural Housing Scotland who has as ever been a source of support, along with Lachie MacDonald. But above all, I want to thank the 'voices' who have contributed the most interesting parts of the book. They are Elizabeth Whitson, Donald Lockhart, Tony Teasdale, Rosemary Williams, Mary

Taylor, Wendy Hebard, Joe Gorman, Neil Clapperton, Peter Hayman and Peter Lee. It has been a real privilege to be able to present their stories. Another key voice is that of Di Alexander who started out as a community activist, has worked in housing and rural development all his days, was for a long time Chair of the Rural and Islands Housing Association Forum, (RIHAF) and has recently been appointed as Chair of the Scottish Rural Fuel Poverty Task Force. He appears in different roles within the overall story. He has written his personal journey, and I think it only appropriate that the book begins with that. It sums up the passion, concern, commitment and ingenuity which characterises many in the sector.

Raymond Young
Dunning
September 2015

You can take the boy out of Colonsay, but you can't take Colonsay out of the boy...

DI ALEXANDER'S JOURNEY

from personal experience to policy expertise . . .

My rural housing journey proper began back in the early 1970s in the Hebridean island of Colonsay. Newly married and with a small baby, we moved into a rented Estate cottage, a whitewashed 'but and ben' with three foot thick stone walls, a slate roof, attic bedrooms that you could hardly stand up in, one you could downstairs, a bathroom with a deep, old-fashioned bath to wallow in, a cosy wee living room with a coal fire plus back boiler for hot water, a pulley over the fireplace to dry the washing on and, finally, a lean-to kitchen tacked on one end with a calor gas cooker and two great Windsor sinks one of which seemed to be permanently full of nappies. It was our first proper home and we quickly became part of a lovely, though fragile, little community. We were so lucky to get such a good start to our newly formed family life and how critically important to it was that affordable *and* available housing opportunity.

I soon became immersed in community living and trying to do something about shared problems like not having mains electricity or water. Then there was housing. Almost every last house was rented from the Estate but as they reduced their workforce, so the houses their former employees left behind were turned into much more remunerative holiday homes. Although full of welcome visitors during the holiday season, most of the year they just stood there looking lifeless. Even more depressing, they were not made available for either those islanders who were making do as best they could in caravans or for some potential new residents like ourselves to move into – we had been the very lucky exceptions to the general rule. The resident population continued its drop by precious drop to decline to an all-time historic low and community confidence suffered.

The inextricable link between the availability of decent, affordable homes and a community's ability to thrive became clear to me: it's so much more than mere bricks and mortar; it's the foremost, fundamental part of the infrastructure required to maintain and develop thriving and self-confident rural communities – particularly the smaller and remoter ones.

The complete lack of an alternative, affordable housing supply just intensified the problem. So, the Community Council lobbied the local authority, Argyll and Bute District Council, to provide some Council housing. Their Chief executive, Michael Gossip, came to have a look for himself and, to our great surprise, told us quite matter-of-factly that the Council had the strategic power to purchase land and/or houses to meet a clear local housing need, compulsorily he added, if that proved necessary. He was then able to persuade the Estate to sell four properties which were turned into welcome and soon filled Council houses. However, what we hadn't woken up to was the equal but opposite surprise that the newly elected Prime Minister had in store for us: it was called the Right to Buy and, as the 1980s unfurled, many rural communities, especially those in popular holiday destinations, began to feel its damaging effect as their small supply of Council houses melted, inexorably, away.

When we moved to the Uists in the early 1980s so that I could manage a newly-formed Community Co-operative, I was astonished to find new, one-off houses springing up everywhere. These were built by crofters who were able to do so because the land was essentially theirs and they didn't have much problem in finding a good house site at little or no cost and then getting Government-funded grant and loan support. It also had much to do with the traditional mind-set i.e. that's what local people were used to doing there to solve their individual housing problem. It was only years later though that I really began to take on board the full significance of the link between the availability of affordable land and affordable housing provision.

Moving back to the mainland as children approached secondary school age, I got a job with Shelter Scotland on a project to persuade owners of empty houses to bring them back into good residential use and condition. It offered empty property owners the chance of an improvement grant, otherwise unavailable to them, if they signed up to the scheme. The incentives worked well and brought flats over shops, empty Estate houses and even some holiday homes back into good and affordable use for people who would otherwise have remained stuck on Council waiting lists. The scheme was successful because the underpinning quid pro quos were well balanced, offering tangible benefits to all parties concerned; but, every bit as importantly, because Government gave revenue funding support to the very labour-intensive – and, inevitably, often abortive – project work involved in finding what is always likely to be a small proportion of genuinely suitable empty homes with genuinely interested owners.

It was plain, though, that in the landward areas of the Highlands, including Lochaber where I was now based, there was a lot more 'hidden' but real-live housing need in the smaller, outlying communities that simply wasn't being recorded on waiting lists or properly recognised. Growing numbers of people, especially younger adults living in old caravans or short-term and sub-standard private lets, felt that there was little point adding their names to the end of lengthy and ever-growing queues for their village council houses which were, in any case, far scarcer, both numerically and proportionately, than they were in the local towns. Whilst not to be discounted, a few, additional empty homes brought back into use weren't ever going to be anywhere near enough to fill the housing gap.

How then to fill it when Councils were not only haemorrhaging houses through Right to Buy sales but, to make matters worse, were effectively being disenfranchised from building new ones because the share of the capital receipts from those Right to Buy sales which they were allowed by Government to keep fell way short of the replacement costs? To add insult to injury, Councils then found themselves stuck for years repaying loans on the very Council houses they had been obliged to sell at astonishingly generous discounts and most local authorities, Lochaber District Council included, had little financial alternative but to stop building houses altogether or they would have gone bust.

But all hope was not necessarily lost. I discovered that there were things called 'community-based housing associations' which in the mid-1980s were still relatively new in Scotland but which had been doing tremendous things in the cities like Glasgow and were beginning to build affordable homes for rent in a few, but by no means all, rural areas. Moreover, they were separately grant-funded by Central Government so brought public funding with them which local authorities did not have to raise themselves. My empty homes work had taken me to Skye where I soon came across the fledgling Lochalsh & Skye Housing Association (LSHA). It was an eye-opener: ordinary local people coming together to set up their own housing association and soon hiring their first Director, Lachie MacDonald, a man with a mission who has been delivering on it ever since. LSHA soon built their first four, new and lovely houses to meet local needs – not, as might have been expected, in the island's capital of Portree but in the distant crofting township of Glendale because the new Association was founded on the belief that the area's housing needs had to be met in the self-same communities they were found in and that meant Glendale's needs were as important as Portree's and, it almost went without saying, would best be met in Glendale rather than Portree – a principle from which LSHA and fellow rural and island associations do not waiver.

If this was what a community-based housing association was all about then why couldn't Lochaber have one too, I wondered? The answer came from the man who ran the Scottish end of The Housing Corporation, the Government body then responsible for funding housing associations – Raymond Young – and he set four tests: provide clear evidence of the local housing need, show real local commitment to forming and sustaining a local housing association, outline a deliverable housing development plan and, finally, prove that the local authority would give a new local housing association 'tangible support'.

The extent of the hidden housing need I had already surveyed and reported on for Shelter in West Lochaber was telling: too many pensioner households or families with small children still living in grossly substandard, damp and expensive private rented housing – some even with no mains water, WCs or electricity – plus a small legion of people, typically young couples, hoping against hope it seemed to get the offer of a local Council house someday, getting through the long Highland winters in condensation traps called caravans, before eventually deciding they had had enough and moving off to Fort William or further where the chances of getting a Council house re-let were so much greater. But then so unlikely, once properly housed, ever to return to the communities they had reluctantly left behind, except as visitors.

The level of local commitment that came forth from every corner of Lochaber for our aspiring Lochaber Housing Association steering group was humbling. The priest, the postmistress, the ambulance driver, the crofter, the family doctor, the hotelier and the local Councillor joined up with off-duty housing and social work officials, 'all united to try and get a locally-based housing association off the ground to give help and hope to the many people we know who are in housing need'. It was personal; they knew and felt for the real, live people stuck in their sub-standard accommodation and they knew and felt too just what it meant to the present and future life of a small rural community to lose a young couple.

Coming up with a prospective housing development plan was the fairly easy bit, securing the 'tangible support' from Lochaber District Council was a bit more challenging. Some of the Councillors were sore that Councils couldn't build houses any more but an upstart housing association apparently could. More difficult to sympathise with was the view expressed to me by one of those unhappy Councillors: 'why on earth do you want to build houses in the back of beyond for, anyway, when everyone knows the need is in the town?' It's a question which sums up a critical element of the perennial rural housing challenge, namely, what's the recipe for getting a predominantly urbanised nation with mainly urban-oriented – small town-oriented can be enough – policy makers and decision-makers to bring the same degree of understanding and commitment to prioritising and solving truly rural housing problems ?

Raymond's recipe was – and remains – the right one: providing really fresh, detailed and credible evidence of the problem; demonstrating a determined and organised coming together of concerned local people to do something about it and uniting behind a well-considered action plan is a fairly unchallengeable basis for eliciting a professional response from responsible professionals no matter how absorbed they are in dealing with other problems. But two other elements are required: good leadership and an engine room. Father Tom Wynne, Lochaber born and bred, man of profound moral resolve combined with unfailing good humour and generosity of spirit, was the ideal leader for our little band of Steering Group enthusiasts and Shelter provided the day to day support needed to keep the engine running. At a tense, climactic meeting of the District Council to consider whether they would back the aspiring local housing association or not, Father Wynne succeeded where even King Canute had failed and turned back the opposing tide – we were going to get our community-based housing association and, another miracle, a new build development programme to go with it. Over twenty-five years and 750 affordable houses later, including many small developments in even the remotest of Lochaber's communities, the decision has been well and truly vindicated.

15

When the handful of rural and island housing associations that were in existence by the late 1980s decided to get together to establish an experience-sharing and lobbying forum (RIHAF) most were only just formed, had minimum staff and had built very few houses between them though they were full of hopes and plans. Since that time they have grown greatly in number and geographical spread and have built thousands of good quality, genuinely affordable homes for local people in housing need in community after rural community, including some of the very smallest, remotest and previously ignored ones like Colonsay itself.

The growth in number is only part of the story: the growth in outreach is much more significant, bringing first hope and, in due course, much-needed new housing to a myriad of small communities the length and breadth of Scotland – places little different from Glendale and Arisaig and Colonsay. Equally important, however, has been the diversification of housing-related activities now carried out by social enterprise subsidiaries set up by housing associations, not least those operating in Scotland's rural and island areas. 'Care and Repair' was one of the earliest and most enduringly successful of examples.

Aimed originally at helping elderly and disabled owner occupiers living in sub-standard houses to get badly needed improvement and adaptations work done to their homes at minimum hassle and cost, the first pioneering projects in Edinburgh and the Western Isles proved so successful that Care & Repair was quickly adopted by a succession of rural and island associations and has since become an integral part of their mainstream work. Several have now added handyperson services which mean that older people can get smaller jobs, like changing a washer, done quickly and well by people they trust. The health care benefits of these caring, person-centred home-delivered services are clear to all involved. My own association in Lochaber has now added a third string and set up a subsidiary, LHA Property Services, which not only provides all the planned maintenance and reactive repair services on LHA stock but offers a similar high quality service to private householders. LHAPS is constituted as a Community Interest Company and covenants profits made back to its charitable parent body, Lochaber HA, and in the process provides skilled trade jobs and apprenticeship opportunities.

Lochalsh & Skye HA's Energy Advice Service has shown that this home-delivered, handholding approach works just as well in helping private sector households living in fuel poverty to reduce the costs of trying to keep their homes warm by pinpointing the home insulation and heating system weaknesses and delivering cost-saving improvements to them. It is also providing hard and accurate evidence of the true extent of the fuel poverty being experienced by those who live in typical rural and island areas and are paying twice as much and more to heat their homes than the national average. Berwickshire HA is pioneering a new and exciting path, which many other associations would also love to follow, by building a three turbine community windfarm generating enough electricity for 4,000 homes and creating a profit-making income stream that will help fund the development of many more affordable rural homes and support many other community projects. Every bit as far-reaching in its potential is the development by a group of urban and rural housing associations which has set up its own company, 'Our Power Energy' and which will supply electricity to housing association customers on better terms than the main utility companies.

Why I believe so deeply in the role played by rural and island housing associations is that, unlike central and local government who shoulder much wider, regional and national strategic responsibilities for every aspect of social and economic welfare and development, local housing associations are able bring a single-minded sense of purpose to solving the housing-related problems of their local communities – the ones in which their staff and volunteer Board members live, know intimately and have their heart.

Rural and island associations only exist because of the decency and commitment of all these unsung heroes and for them I offer just one example, Catriona Macmillan, a founder member of Lochaber HA, who ran the Post Office from her home in Kilchoan at the far end of the Ardnamurchan peninsula. Summer and winter, year in year out, Catriona would finish work and drive to Fort William to contribute her wisdom and good grace to Board meetings, which not infrequently ended at 10 o clock at night, before setting off on the long and tortuous single track road back home again. Catriona saw nothing particularly remarkable about her commitment, freely and happily given, because it was simply what you needed to do, not just for your own village but equally for the wider local community of which you were a part.

Nevertheless, such unassuming dedication is the very essence of rural and island housing associations and explains why they are not inclined to shy away from tackling what to others might seem like remote and unduly troublesome local housing problems – and, as a result, deliver the prize of good, local housing solutions where they would, in my experience, be far less likely to be delivered otherwise.

The role and local impact of rural and island housing associations feature large in my own housing journey not because I don't think local authorities and central government don't care about or contribute greatly to delivering good solutions to affordable housing problems in rural Scotland – they clearly do and, given a fair political wind, will continue so to do. In any event, housing associations, trusts and the like can only operate successfully on the basis of support from and genuine partnership-working with local and national government. Each of these three main players brings something different and unique to the table and the complementarity of their differing roles is generally well understood and respected by those involved.

However, whilst housing associations, trusts and some representative bodies like Shelter and RIHAF – as well as, to a degree, rural communities themselves – can exert some useful influence on rural housing policy development, the actual power to alter its direction of travel, to create or remove strategic roadblocks to it – like the controversial Right to Buy policy now, thankfully, all but consigned to the history books – lies first and foremost with central government. Like others I was suspicious as well as surprised when, at the end of the 1980s, the same Prime Minister who had introduced the Right to Buy then created a new Government housing agency called Scottish Homes. I was much better pleased, though, when the very first new policy Scottish Homes announced it would focus on was its Rural Housing Policy which it consulted upon widely and unveiled in 1990.

At long last and following well-evidenced reports from organisations like Rural Forum and Shelter Scotland, rural housing issues were being given the serious attention they had long deserved but not really received – and wouldn't have even then without the determination shown by the new policy's progenitor, Raymond Young. It proposed carefully considered remedies to evident policy gaps, the most significant of which for me was a new approach to encouraging self-build/self-commissioned housing with a brand new grant to match. Registered crofters had long been able to access their Government grant and a loan scheme to help them build new homes for themselves and it had been successfully delivering well over a hundred new croft houses a year in some of the remotest rural communities in the Highlands & Islands. Moreover, it was providing excellent value for public money as it was delivering three new houses for the same amount of public investment it took to build just one housing association or council house for rent.

Now a similar grant incentive (minus the additional loan element), known as a Rural Home Ownership Grant or RHOG as it soon became known, was to be made available to non-crofters who aspired to solve their housing problems by building a modest home for themselves. They would be required to prove, though, that they wouldn't be able to afford to do so without additional financial assistance – the RHOG coming in to fill the gap between what they could raise themselves, by way of savings plus a mortgage, and their overall outlay in buying a plot and getting the house built. They would also be required to live in the house for ten years or, if not, they would have to pay the RHOG back in full to Scottish Homes.

It was a truly imaginative policy leap. That constant harvest of croft houses, which I had been amazed to see springing up in the Uists, also supported a thriving local building industry which, in turn, was providing a social and economic double whammy for the community thereby adding great value for the public money invested. Surely RHOGs would now be able to deliver the same benefits but more widely?

The answer was definitely yes, though one or two serious buts gradually became apparent. RHOGs worked particularly well in many parts of the Highlands & Islands whilst they had little or no impact in other parts of rural Scotland, not least because they received nothing like the same level of recognition and support from the regional Scottish Homes offices responsible for promoting them. But there was a more fundamental problem – first finding a plot to build on and then finding the ever-increasing price of purchasing it.

The difference in the take-up of the respective building grants by crofters and non-crofters and between crofting and non-crofting areas became clearer: crofters had little difficulty finding a house site on their croft land which cost them virtually nothing apart from the cost of developing it; the non-crofter, on the other hand, would have to find a plot which someone else owned and then persuade them to sell it to them cheaply if they were then going to be able to afford the overall cost of building even a modest home, even with the help of a RHOG. This kind of leg-up was and is much more likely to happen in crofting areas where a multiplicity of crofters have ownership or equivalent rights over small but significant acreages of land and may also be willing to help other family members and, to a lesser extent, other members of the community secure a house plot at a genuinely affordable purchase price.

If, however, like the great majority of people living in rural or even crofting areas you don't happen to have inside track with an obliging owner of a cheap plot then you only have the open market to fall back on. But even back in the 1990s, long before the housing market set off on its stratospheric price rise journey that crashed back to earth in 2008, finding affordable and economically developable land for locally affordable housing was still a struggle, whether it was individuals seeking RHOG plots for one-off houses or rural housing associations seeking sites for small developments. *And* the site acquisition costs, when added to the ground works and building costs, were generally way beyond the means of ordinary working people. What could be done in a practical way to make things easier?

Strategic landbanking seemed to me to offer an answer. I became convinced that being able to guarantee an advance supply of real live, suitably located, readily available, affordable-to-purchase, affordable-to-develop sites was the key to ensuring the provision of affordable rural housing – in whichever communities both the need and the type of housing best suited to meeting that need are identified. Even if the public investment wasn't immediately available to support the affordable housing provision for which the site had been purchased/landbanked, the site would be sitting there ready and waiting when it was. Experience showed, however, that it was much easier for a rural community to interest the key affordable housing funders and developers – central and local government, local housing associations, aspiring RHOG-assisted self-builders – in prioritising and delivering some affordable housing if they knew that the obstacle of securing a suitable housing site or house plot had already been cleared out of their way.

So I put forward a proposal for a new type of partnership vehicle – The Highlands Small Communities Housing Trust (HSCHT) – which would help the affordable housing system work better for the rural communities of the Highlands by undertaking strategic landbanking on their behalf. It would ultimately be owned by the rural and island communities whose needs it was set up to serve but the composition and balance of its Board and advisory members would ensure that all the main stakeholders shared equally in its discussions and decisions – Scottish Government, Highlands & Islands Enterprise, the local housing associations, the organisations representing both Scottish landowners and crofters, Community Councils and, crucially, the local authority, Highland Council, without whose moral and funding support the Trust would never have got off the ground.

Though there was little difficulty in persuading any of the partners to sign up to HSCHT's widely supported cause, there are always some key individuals who you very much need to have on your side. None more so than Jill Stewart, Highland Council's then Head of Housing Strategy, who not only gave it her wholehearted backing but was then responsible for making a successful pitch for a very much one off Scottish Government Challenge Fund grant of £1.4 million to enable the Trust to set up a 'revolving' landbanking' fund. It revolves because it is regularly replenished by the proceeds of subsequent site and plot sales, thus allowing the land-bank fund to keep rolling over on a cyclical basis, the main restriction being the size of the capital in the landbanking fund that is available to work with.

The new vehicle was now able to put theory into practice and it worked: sites were bought in needy communities across the Highlands with some being sold to local Housing Associations, like Albyn Housing Society, who as a result, were able to build small schemes of affordable rented housing in small community after small community in previously deprived parts of the Highlands like Wester Ross. Other sites or parts of sites were turned into serviced house plots which were sold to people, typically young couples, who were just able to afford to build a home for themselves with the help of both the RHOG and the plot provided by the Trust at much less than market value.

This then raised another critical issue: how to persuade landowners to sell economically developable and otherwise suitable sites cheaply so that HSCHT could then, in its turn, sell them on at the cheap prices needed to make them viable for those aspiring RHOG plot purchasers? It's not that most landowners aren't sympathetically inclined towards helping the rural communities of which they are a part; they just don't jump at the idea of finding themselves ripped off a few years down the line by a plot purchaser building a nice detached house on it but then deciding to move on and sell up – and, as a result, pocketing the full and enhanced market value of the plot which the landowner had generously sold at a discount believing it was to help the community meet their long-term affordable housing needs rather than gift an unintended windfall to the lucky plot purchaser. Landowners were, not unreasonably, seeking some cast iron reassurances and weren't inclined to be fobbed off with vague answers.

As with accessing the public money to create the landbanking fund, HSCHT found itself in the right place at the right time again to help put another theory to the practical test. The new Scottish Parliament was busy passing land reform legislation and their proposals to sweep away outmoded title conditions nevertheless included some exceptions, known as 'burdens', to protect particular areas of public interest like conservation. To help persuade landowners to sell sites cheaply we proposed adding a 'Rural Housing Burden' (RHB) which would lock the discounted value of the land price into the title to the property *in perpetuity* as an affordability dividend that would benefit not just the first owner of the plot on the site but every subsequent owner. So, for example, if the discounted land price brings the total plot development costs down by 25% then, as and when the owner of the house built on the site sells it, the purchase price for the next owner would be discounted to 75% of full market value. Only bona fide affordable rural housing bodies can use this RHB mechanism which has since proved its effectiveness in both persuading owners to sell sites cheaply and assisting local people who would not otherwise have been able to afford to build or buy a home of their own locally.

In my view though, the Rural Housing Burden still has considerable potential to influence the future direction of travel of rural housing policy for the better in that it offers a unique means of protection for any additional grants or discounts offered to bring rural home ownership within the financial means of ordinary local people, particularly those young couples who want to go living and raising families in their preferred communities. The late and much lamented RHOG, which, mistakenly in the view of many rural housing practitioners, has currently been shelved by Government, more than deserves a comeback. However, when it does, it also deserves to be protected by the Rural Housing Burden. This way Scottish Government and society could be sure that the grant would not only benefit the first recipient but would also provide much longer term benefit to subsequent purchasers who will have equal need of some 'affordability' assistance.

Rural housing policy and matching public investment must, of course, address other needs, not least those of the majority of households who currently have no other affordable option than housing for rent, but the road to successful affordable housing development is so littered with obstacles that it is often a wonder and a tribute to the terrier-like tenacity of the developers that anything gets built at all. Finding a decent site | With a potentially willing seller | Well enough located and economically developable | Peat and/or rock a particular rural speciality | Legal issues another, which only reveal themselves when the Title to the land can be thoroughly scrutinised | Infrastructure and site servicing issues | Water and sewerage constraints | Site access and Roads Dept. requirements | Other Planning Permission requirements | Environmental surveys | Archaeological surveys | Ground contamination surveys | Flood risk surveys | 'Planning gain' requirements | Negotiating a sensible purchase price, all things considered | Getting community support and dealing with NIMBY concerns | Securing the public funding required | From different funders | Securing the supplementary private finance required from lenders and on terms which don't finish you off | Finding a good builder | Dealing with the totally unforeseeable once you start developing the site e.g. builder going bust.

Each issue in this non-exhaustive list is worth a separate chapter and, given a good networking opportunity, can keep rural housing providers comparing horror stories late into the night. How to deal with them all as efficiently and positively as possible was the question which a now all but forgotten Scottish Government instigated initiative, called Rural Partnership For Change, asked as the noughties replaced the nineties and it came up with one particularly good and practical answer – as beneficial, in my view, as any single improvement in rural housing practice in the last thirty years.

Rural Housing Development Forums were the brainchild of the Initiative's Highland Pilot group. They were designed to get all the key players who are involved in facilitating and delivering new and affordable rural housing, of whatever type and mix, to come together regularly for at least four or five several hour long meetings each year. There they were charged with the professional responsibility of *collectively* considering, on a community by community and site by site basis, all the obstacles standing in the way of a proposed affordable housing development, how best to get round them and who needed to do what to get the desired outcome. The list of expected participants was as broad as the housing-related develop-ment issues involved required and included the most senior staff from the

Council's housing development, roads, both Planning Office and Local Plan departments, local housing associations and housing trusts, Scottish Water, SEPA and Highlands & Islands Enterprise plus sometimes other invitees who could bring additional know-how to bear upon particular issues of concern. There were six different Development Forums covering the various distinct geographical areas of the Highlands so the membership at each meeting varied according to which professional had the in-depth local knowledge and lead responsibility for the particular locality.

These Council led Housing Development Forums quickly proved a more effective and agreeable way of getting results than the previous much more restricted and ad hoc way of doing business. Detailed, site-specific knowledge was shared regularly, openly and collaboratively and the professionals, some of whom might previously have been prone to a bit of 'silo mentality', not only forgot it and developed a much better understanding of other's experience and concerns but then made the extra effort required between meetings to deal with action points arising so that they could look and feel good reporting back positively to the next one. Yes, tensions might occasionally show but generally the meetings were characterised by a greatly improved communication, good humour and a much increased appreciation that the process was about a joint commitment to problem solving. The Forums went into temporary abeyance as the recession hit housing development hard but have now been re-instigated as a regular component in the partnership-working approach to affordable housing delivery that has proved so productive for the Highlands over many years.

I look back on the rural housing journey I have made trying to help rural communities find good solutions to their affordable housing problems and ask myself what real advances in both policy and practice have been made and what the future might hold. My short answer is that though some really significant progress has been made on some fronts, there's a long way still to go on others.

Based on front-line experience, many rural housing practitioners share the belief that it serves the interests of rural communities better to have more policy mechanisms than less available to address housing problems because the customer-tailored, 'horses for courses' approach improves take-up in subtly differing rural housing markets, each with its unique set of demographic, social and economic development needs and aspirations.

Where one household may prefer shared ownership to shared equity or vice versa, another truly aspires to build their own home if they could get an affordable house plot and a bit of grant support. And if you listen to what individual communities are saying as the customers, some have already made it clear that they would prefer to build, own and allocate their own affordable homes if they could get a grant, like the Scottish Governments' successful but since shelved Rural Homes for Rent scheme, rather than have to wait for their Council or local housing association to do it.

Which raises the biggest challenge of all for the future development and direction of travel for affordable rural housing policy: why in this day and age, shouldn't Scotland's rural communities be given *real*, i.e. solid, meaningful, grown-up, control over their own, individual developmental destinies, not least their housing destinies, rather than never really being quite trusted enough to be more than just enthusiastic consultees whose views and judgements may or may not be taken on board and, when push comes to shove, may well end up being side-lined by private or public interests which are accorded greater precedence in the present pecking order? Other nations happily devolve a much greater level of democratic responsibility and solid, local decision-making power down to small communities without having brought on the end of civilisation as it is known locally by countries such as France, Switzerland and Norway. Indeed, the lesson to be drawn from those Scottish rural communities, like Knoydart and Helmsdale, which have taken land into community ownership and used it to build their own affordable housing assets to meet local needs, is that the experience transforms their sense of self-belief and makes them much less inclined to sit back and wait for some well-intentioned but still outside interest to do it for them. Helmsdale had been asking but waiting thirty-five years for some new and affordable houses before they took matters into their own hands and, having now successfully built their first four houses, are confidently planning a second phase.

It is, of course, essential that all interested parties, not least local landowners and Planning Departments and potential affordable housing providers, feed their important considerations into the decision-making process but the *ultimate* decision should lie with the community, on the grounds that the provision and location of affordable housing for the purpose of sustainable community development should now be treated as the normal and inalienable, aspirational ambition of any community: one that may not be unreasonably blocked by any other interest or interest group within or beyond that community, provided due and proper process has been followed in reaching a collectively and properly agreed view on the matter.

I hold this view because of the many communities and community groups I have had contact with in my career as a rural housing adviser and enabler – all those meetings in village halls, most of them public and often amazingly well-attended by local residents, young, old and in between, who need no lessons on how important the provision of affordable housing is to the well-being of their community which, whatever its local quirks, they know and love best. Nor do they lack the appetite or the ability to understand the key issues involved and reach an informed consensus, notwithstanding the challenges involved, on what they want to see happen next. Some, like Helmsdale and Knoydart, have already proved that small, even very small, communities are up for the challenge of taking the direct asset-owning (first the land, then the houses) route to solving their local housing problems themselves. Others have shown they are interested in the possibilities, particularly if it was easier for them to acquire key sites and if other communities are not yet particularly interested in such asset-owning challenges and responsibilities then they may wish to change their mind in the future and should, therefore, be accorded the same rights to do so.

Plenty of careful thought is required to sort out the detail of the 'due and proper process' involved in transferring such authority to rural communities and more will be required to ensure that the principle of 'sustainable community development' cannot be hijacked by factions within communities who are resistant to affordable housing development. It would not be good enough, however, to cry 'NIMBY' and ignore any objections expressed within the community to a particular affordable housing proposal: the community's grown-up responsibility would be to demonstrate that the proposal could provide satisfactory answers to each objection by reference to criteria which describe 'sustainable, affordable housing development' as well as to clear evidence of the housing-related community development need for it.

However, empowering communities to take asset-owning control over solving local housing problems requires funding and expertise, as well as new rights. Whilst the re-launched Scottish Land Fund has great and very welcome potential to help communities fund the land and other asset purchases they need to realise their affordable housing and other community development ambitions, the opportunity remains to put in place a complementary Government-backed funding stream to encourage and help the next generation of Helmsdales and Knoydarts to meet the considerable capital costs involved in then being able to build affordable houses on the land they come to own.

The innovative CLT (Community Land Trust) model now operating south of the Border offers English rural communities the structured funding routes and expert advice they need to do what those bold and pathfinding Scottish rural communities have done on a more ad hoc basis, albeit with very similar partnership support from local landowners, local housing associations, housing trusts and local authorities. From my personal perspective, I see particular benefits flowing from the now tried and tested English housing association/CLT partnering model whereby communities draw on the local housing association's or regional housing trust's housing development and financial management know-how to help them reduce the pain and difficulty of actually building the affordable houses they want to have but without usurping the community's right, through its CLT, to retain the ownership and ultimate control over the land the houses are built on and, as a consequence, the ownership, use and destiny of the houses themselves and the ordinary members of the community whose needs they exist to serve.

So when I look back on the road I've travelled on my own rural housing journey – much of it single track – I see real changes for the better in understanding and policy and practice. And when I imagine what the road ahead may look like beyond the visible horizon I see many, many more individual communities owning pieces of land, building affordable houses and taking charge of their usage to fulfil their community development aims – not instead of housing provided by Councils, housing associations and private landlords, all of which has a continuingly important part to play, but as a community-empowering addition to its critically important asset base of affordable housing to meet local needs. I look forward to the next stages in the journey and, hopefully, seeing it happen.

PART ONE

The Overview

CHAPTER ONE

2015

Rural Scotland and affordable housing

Rural Scotland is marketed as an idyllic place – soaring mountains, deep lochs, romantic passes, high quality arable land, beautiful towns and scattered crofts. It is all of these things – and many people come to visit because of them. It has also attracted many people to come and live in the countryside. Unlike many other developed countries, Scotland is enjoying an increase in population in its rural communities – including in some of the most remote areas. The lifestyle may be what many people want; and different people seek different lifestyles. For many it is an escape from the hustle and bustle of the big cities – they seek quiet and want to live the dream they have hankered after for years. For some it is a combination of living in the countryside while commuting to a city job. For others it is an opportunity to bring up a family in an area where commuting is not required, in what is perceived as a crime free environment and where the community is made up of people who look out for one another. While for others it is an opportunity to return to their family roots, or an opportunity to develop land or sea based employment. Rural Scotland means many things to many people.

However, growth brings its own challenges. Rural development in Scotland is carefully managed. The one common factor to all those who live in the countryside is that everyone needs a place to live. The views may be spectacular. But you can't live in a view. If you have plenty of money you will have little difficulty in purchasing a house or buying land and build one. Indeed you may well outbid someone on modest or low income. Affordable housing to rent or buy remains in very short supply. And thus, particularly if you are young, you may find yourself having to stay with relatives, sleeping on a friend's floor or a caravan. Or you may have to abandon your plan to work and live in the countryside. In areas where tourism is the main industry you may be able to rent a house for the winter, but have to find somewhere to live during 'the season'. And those on 'modest incomes' can include the teacher, the nurse, the fisherman, the plumber, the joiner, the chef and the hotel receptionist. Key jobs to ensure the economic and social future of rural Scotland.

Affordable housing comes in three types – home ownership, rent from the private sector, or rent from a social housing landlord. All three suffer from pressure, where demand outstrips supply. In the social housing sector, the major player providing new lettings over the last twenty-five years has been the housing association, or as it is now known as the Registered Social Landlord.

Housing associations have a long history. Their origins can be traced back to almshouses with further development in the nineteenth century through philanthropic and voluntary organisations responding to the atrocious housing conditions found in cities in the wake of the industrial revolution. There was a significant growth period in the second half of the twentieth century, including many of whose stories will be told in this book. Housing associations are non-profit organisations run by a volunteer committee, which in most cases is elected from a membership that is open to tenants, individual members of the public and community organisations, as well as to other stakeholders and partners.

In rural Scotland, housing associations come in three varieties – locally based, covering perhaps a few settlements within a recognisable rural area; regional, with its head office in a rural town but covering a wider area; and national, mainly providing housing for specific groups of people – e.g. elderly. Some of them have grown slowly over the years; others have appeared very quickly but with a housing stock that goes back years, having taken over public sector housing.

So while this book starts with an introduction to the history of rural housing over the last 200 years or so, it will concentrate on the development of rural based housing associations over the last thirty years and within the context of housing policy as it affected rural Scotland.

What is meant by rural Scotland? Is it simply non-urban? Is a definition important? It seems to be as it has been the subject of much debate over the years. It is needed for analysis, for policy making, for resource distribution, and therefore for understanding the differences in social structures, demands and needs from urban communities. Without it no one can be sure that the investment is getting to the people and places that

A small development makes a huge difference to a rural community.
Lochalsh and Skye Housing Association development on Raasay.
Photo: Lochalsh and Skye Housing Association

The tourist view of rural Scotland in 2015 – Iona.
Photo: Raymond Young

In 2015 you can get a bus to Iona – there is work, but the drivers have to live
in a caravan in the bus yard since there are not enough houses on Mull.

Photo: Jodi MacLeod, Our Island Home Project, Rural Housing Scotland

The launch of the Scottish Homes Rural Housing Policy in September 1990 –
Princess Anne with Sir James Mellon, John Richards, Heather Sheerin, Raymond Young.

Photo: Scottish Homes collection

What it is all about – Albyn Housing Society's happy new tenants.
Photo: Albyn Housing Society

Orkney Housing Association's development at St Mary's, Holm.
Photo: Orkney Housing Association

The future? Dunbritton Housing Association's Silverhills Housing, Roseneath. An award winning innovative affordable rural housing development with flexible, home, work layouts. The buildings are based on the narrow plans and proportions of traditional rural houses. They benefit from passive solar gain during winter months with southwest facing orientation and incorporate solar water heating tiles. Architect Anderson Bell+Christie.

Photo: Dunbritton Housing Association

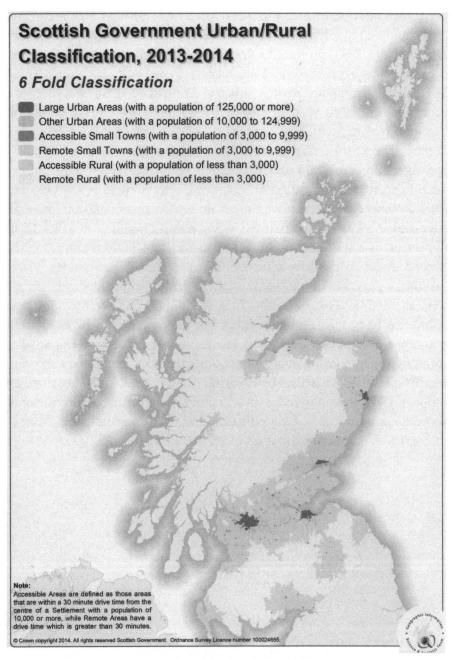

Scottish Government Urban/Rural Classification, 2013-2014

6 Fold Classification

- Large Urban Areas (with a population of 125,000 or more)
- Other Urban Areas (with a population of 10,000 to 124,999)
- Accessible Small Towns (with a population of 3,000 to 9,999)
- Remote Small Towns (with a population of 3,000 to 9,999)
- Accessible Rural (with a population of less than 3,000)
- Remote Rural (with a population of less than 3,000)

Note:
Accessible Areas are defined as those areas that are within a 30 minute drive time from the centre of a Settlement with a population of 10,000 or more, while Remote Areas have a drive time which is greater than 30 minutes.

© Crown copyright 2014. All rights reserved Scottish Government. Ordnance Survey Licence number 100024655.

Urban/rural classification 2013–2014 map.
By permission of the Scottish Government

need it. In the Countryside (Scotland) Act 1967, 98% of Scotland's land area could be regarded as rural. In 1978 the then Scottish Development Department (SDD) produced a definition of urban, rural and remote, the definition was applied to the then relatively new District Council areas. There were many anomalies in it – such as Arran being urban and Inverness being rural. In 1990 Scottish Homes tried a more fine grained definition based on parishes with a population density of less than one person per hectare. The Scottish Government Urban Rural Classification (SGURC) was introduced in 2000 and is updated every two years. This defines settlements with a population of 3,000 or less to be rural. It also classifies areas as remote based on drive time from settlements of 10,000 or more. Accessible Areas are those that are within a thirty minute drive time from the centre of a settlement with a population of 10,000 or more, while Remote Areas have a drive time that is greater than thirty minutes.

For the purposes of this book, all these definitions will be used as they were at the time. For future thoughts the SGURC will suffice, although 3,000 may be too large in many cases. For the purposes of this book rural housing is about good quality affordable accommodation in our smaller communities, often providing a few homes that can help that community remain sustainable, whether by ensuring economic sustainability through supporting local employment, by ensuring social sustainability through keeping communities together, or ensuring environmental sustainability through well managed natural resources.

CHAPTER TWO

1984

A forgotten problem?

The date 1984 will always be associated with a book that was written in the remote Argyllshire island of Jura. Orwell's description of a world of constant war, deception and totalitarian control may have been seen as a world away from the remoteness of Jura when it was written in 1948. By happenchance, 1984 was the year in which a small Scottish organisation, Rural Forum, exposed the hidden, what they called 'forgotten', problem of rural housing. There was no suggestion that deception or totalitarian control had hidden the problem, more like that it had been forgotten against the huge urban challenges that had been the focus for successions of governments, housing agencies and lobby groups.

Rural Forum was an alliance of organisations that represented people living and working in the Scottish Countryside. It promoted rural concerns, provided services to rural communities, and published reports, including *'Scotland's Rural Housing – a forgotten problem'*. The Forum's

Jura.

Housing Working Group included people who would make a significant contribution to rural policy and development over the years – including Jim Hunter, the historian and journalist who would steer the Scottish Crofters Union and then Highlands and Islands Enterprise into the twenty-first century and Mark Shucksmith, then a lecturer who would become the UK's foremost rural researcher and commentator and who would chair the early twenty-first century Crofting review

Reading the report thirty years later one realises that despite all the efforts, some of the key problems remain. Its three main concerns were:

- The poor physical condition of the housing stock
- The lack of accommodation for those on lower incomes
- The financial cutbacks that had reduced new construction

They also identified some specific issues that affected rural Scotland – crofter housing, tied housing, holiday accommodation, and agriculture rents. And significantly – at least to this author – they stated that *there is evidence that rural development is hampered by housing problems*', reinforcing the view of the Highlands and Islands Development Board in 1974.

A brief history leading up to the 1984 report

Before looking at the 1984 report in more detail it may be worth asking – why had the rural housing become the 'forgotten problem'? Most of the analysis on rural housing is about the 'what' – the state of the stock, homeless figures, land prices etc. At the risk of recounting old stories, it is useful to understand why the issue is 'forgotten'. So what follows is one version. As usual with history (especially potted histories) there is a bias in the recounting.

Over the nineteenth and twentieth centuries Scotland had been one of the fastest urbanising nations in the world. Its place at the heart of the industrial revolution meant that the demand for (cheap) labour in its burgeoning cities made it attractive for immigrants. And the industrial revolution accompanied by the transport infrastructural changes also applied to what had been an agricultural based nation. It applied to the supporting industries as well – smaller local quarries, metal working, and supply chains. Agricultural changes in farming led to depopulation across the country. In some places whole communities were moved to make way for new agricultural practices and while the Highland Clearances have a particular resonance and notoriety for most of us (and may have seen some of the worst examples of landlord and factor inhumanity), the depopulation applied right across the countryside. Sometimes statistics don't capture the position and it is left to storytellers to help us understand the reality and to give us the flavour of the impact of the changes on people's lives. James Barke's book *Land of the Leal*, which describes a family's journey from agricultural poverty and tenancy in the Whinns of Galloway in the South West, through Fife and into the harsh urban environment of Glasgow in the early twentieth century, along with the better known *Scots Quair* which tells the story of Chris Guthrie and the changes in her life from rural North East through the First World War and into the city, gives a picture of the impact of the agricultural changes outside Gàidhealtachd.

With rural immigrants cramming into the cities, the housing condition of urban dwellers became the focus of housing reformers in the nineteenth century. The prevailing attitude would be that rural Scotland was depopulating; there were fewer people to be concerned about. The Highlands were being taken over by sheep and sporting estates. Land ownership has always been controlled by a few – clan estates forfeited by the crown after the Jacobite rebellion had been distributed to the favoured landowners; while elsewhere in Scotland, larger estates were part of the rationalisation of agriculture. And in both, there was little or no security of tenure for those who did not own land. So the system was stacked against those with low incomes. (We may castigate – rightly – those who took advantage of the system and abused it. But the system itself bred abuse)

There were, however, events that did force governments to face up to some the facts. First there was a series of disturbances in what came to be known as the crofting counties. Martin Luther King Jnr described riots as 'the language of the unheard'. And that could easily have applied to crofters in Skye as to the black poor in Newark, New Jersey. Maybe the word 'riot' is too strong to describe the disturbances by crofter and cottars in the 1870s but the feeling of being 'unheard' led to demonstrations against excessively high rents, lack of security and forced evictions. A stand had to be made. The police reported that they found it difficult to cope with the increasing demands placed upon them when called by landlords to enforce what the landlords believed were their rights. Gladstone's Government, faced with civil disturbance in Ireland and some 140 years after the '45, reacted by setting up the Royal Commission of Inquiry into the Conditions of Crofters and Cottars in the Highlands and Islands. The Commission, nearly every member of which was himself a landowner, held hearings starting in Skye and visited communities the length and breadth of the Highlands and Islands, gathering evidence from crofters, landlords and others familiar with the conditions of rural communities. It worked quickly and reported in 1884, providing a fascinating record of life in that part of rural Scotland. It may have contributed to the legislation of 1886 – the Crofters' Holdings (Scotland) Act – although there remain some questions about its direct impact. It did, however, raise the issues. The legislation provided for the first time some security of tenure in the seven crofting counties covering the Western seaboard and the Northern Isles. But it did not solve the problems, with more trouble through the early twentieth century, and the need for more legislation. One of the outcomes of the crofting legislation as it developed over the years was an unique part of the Department of Agriculture and Fisheries (DAFS) which provided advice, housing design and financial support for crofters, along with material depots that enabled some crofters to build good quality housing.

But Parliament was faced with greater housing concerns than crofters. In 1912, another Royal Commission was set up, in response to concerns raised about the housing conditions of miners, including deputations from the Scottish Miners' Federation. This, the Royal Commission on the Housing of the Industrial Population of Scotland Rural and Urban took evidence across the country, including rural mining areas like the Fife mining villages, fishing villages in the north east, crofting townships and 'Outer Hebridean Areas'. The Commissioners were shocked by the living conditions, whether in Glasgow or in rural areas. *'The housing conditions in Lewis are deplorable . . . in many the cattle are housed under the same roof as the human beings . . . as the manure from the byre is removed once a year, the conditions can be better imagined than described . . .'* Evidence was taken until 1915, but the work of the Commission was suspended for a year during the War, with the report being published in 1917.

Meanwhile, during the war, rent strikes, led by women as a result of landlords taking advantage of war shortages and absent workers, had worried the Government, including creating nervousness about a possible Bolshevik revolution in Clydeside. Urban housing had to be a priority.

The Royal Commission can be seen as one of the major spurs to the fundamental changes that took place in Scotland's housing after WW1 with the growth of local authorities in place of the private sector as the principal provider of new homes. Inevitably, with the scale of the urban challenge, resources and legislation were targeted to the overcrowded cities. Some local authority housing was provided in rural areas and the Government's own housing developer, Scottish Special Housing Association (SSHA), was to contribute where large scale economic development was being undertaken like Invergordon or Fort William.

After the Second World War, urban Scotland still dominated housing policy. Rural areas continued to experience population decline. Young people moved to the cities for further education and did not move back because the kind of employment they wanted or were skilled for did not exist. Agriculture continued to mechanise and involve fewer people. The travellers who had moved with the seasons working on the land became house dwellers and moved into the towns. The herring fishing fleets had declined and with them the fisherwomen who had moved round the coasts following the shoals. The arrival of cars, which more and more people could access, along with changes in retail saw the closure of local shops, as journeys to towns and supermarkets became more possible. Rural Scotland as place to live and work seemed almost in terminal decline, although 'hunting, shooting and fishing' continued to grow, along with the use of the countryside for general recreation.

But fortunes were changing. With the creation of the North of Scotland Hydro Electric Board, Tom Johnston, then Secretary of State for Scotland, hoped that the Board would lead to economic revival in the Highlands. While the immediate economic impact did not happen, what did happen was that there was major social benefit by bringing power – at considerable expense – to far-flung Highland communities. The Hydro was followed by the Highland Panel in 1951, which was then replaced in 1964 by the Highlands and Islands Development Board (HIDB) with the aim of encouraging economic and social development of the Highlands and Islands. And soon the HIDB was warning that a lack of available housing was holding up and preventing development projects in their area, because potential employers could not find accommodation for themselves or their key workers. HIDB also reported that the lack of housing caused young people to leave their home areas and migrate elsewhere. It had commissioned a number of reports about housing within its area. For example, in one *Housing Improvement Surveys Barra 1972* (undertaken by a group of architects from Strathclyde University) which highlighted the poor physical condition of the housing stock, the Board foreword included *'For a number of years the Board has been conscious of acute housing problems in some of the remoter parts of the Highlands and Islands. Initially this stemmed mainly from the difficulty in finding suitable housing for workers in development projects assisted by the Board. Although no houses could be easily obtained for new workers, a casual examination appeared to reveal empty houses which were of adequate standard or could be improved to adequate standard . . . Provision of housing is within the jurisdiction of the local authorities. Yet the Board is inevitably involved – lack of housing can frustrate development, and poor housing can be a serious social handicap.'*

While the Highlands and Islands were the emotional and planning focus – partly because of a series of romantic writers starting with Walter Scott and through to historical authors like John Prebble, partly because of the strength of the Gàidhealtachd diaspora, and perhaps more than a little collective guilt about the clearances, the rest of rural Scotland tended to lag behind. There was no special legislation for farm tenants like that for crofters, no financial schemes like those offered by DAFS, and (unlike HIDB) no social powers for the Scottish Development Agency (SDA) which inevitably concentrated its energies on big developments – oil, city reconstruction and manufacturing decline – and said little about the role of housing in rural development.

While access to housing was one issue, the condition of the stock was another. In 1967, the Scottish Housing Advisory Committee (the Cullingworth Report) was horrified to discover that housing conditions in rural areas were even worse than those of Glasgow and other inner cities. The committee criticised local councils *'the problem is not being tackled with the urgency it deserves'*.

The Rural Forum Report and its impact

It was against this background that Rural Forum produced its report. At that time, few documents had produced such a comprehensive review of rural housing in Scotland. The working group included Councillors, local authority housing directors, representatives of the strategic planners in Regional Councils, housing associations, Shelter, HIDB with observers from the Scottish Development Department and the Housing Corporation (including your author). The report still stands as a major contribution; the basis of some of the major decisions that were to come, even if it took some time to work its way through the political processes. It set out to analyse the then current state of rural housing drawing upon the latest (quite voluminous) research and quoting examples. Rather than recommending solutions, it posed a series of questions. It was called 'a discussion paper'. Very few copies still exist. It was typed and produced 'in house'. So there is no apology for extracting much of its content. It is a foundational document for rural housing policy and for many rural housing associations.

Rural Forum report cover.

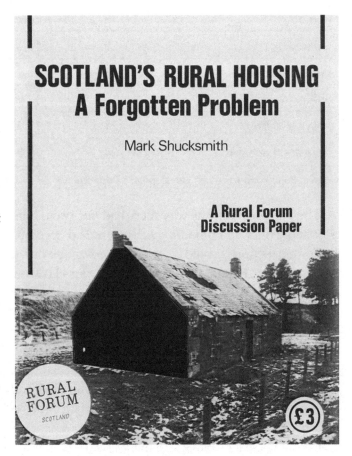

House condition

The report began with a review of the condition of the housing stock following the Cullingworth Report. Improvements had been made since 1967. Using the statutory definition 'Below Tolerable Standard' (BTS) introduced in 1969 and revised in 1974, the report set the change between 1976 and 1982:

	1976 (%)	1982 (%)	Change (%)
Scotland	8	4.5	-46
Rural and remote Scotland	9	6.0	-32
Remote	13	9.5	-29
Orkney	29	15.6	-46
Western Isles	31	23.0	-26
Shetland	19	15.1	-21
Argyll and Bute	21	17.1	-19
Skye and Lochalsh	24	19.5	-19

(Source: Rural Forum/Scottish Development Department)

The big question was why there had not been a similar change in rural Scotland. Policy and funding mechanisms had been provided in legislation. Improvement grants could be given, improvement orders issued, or Housing Action Areas (HAAs) declared. But, as the HIDB noted *the admirable concept of HAAs appears to have been designed with city blocks in mind*. And they were. Your author's book *Annie's Loo* tells how HAAs were success-fully used for tenements in urban council areas after some experimentation with procedures and partnerships. Some rural authorities tried the challenge of HAAs. Western Isles was creative and declared HAAs in townships where houses were hundreds of metres apart. Argyll and Bute had sufficient tenements to apply the HAA legislation, but had difficulty in improving more remote dwellings. One of the advantages of HAAs was that a higher level of grant could be paid. But Government's own research showed that the cost of repairs was proportionately higher in rural areas, and increased with remoteness. Something that would become, and remains today, a recurring theme.

If the HAA process was not designed for rural areas, what about improvement grants and orders? These too suffered from higher costs but with lower levels of grant available. But that was not all the story. Much of the BTS housing was occupied by elderly people on low incomes. Indeed one of the characteristics of rural communities is lower incomes and higher living costs. The ability to access loans may create a financial hurdle, but there were other factors as well. Many older people did not want to face the upheaval of a major building operation. As an HIDB report noted '*in many cases what is wanted is something quite minor and simple which, to them, would make an enormous difference to their lives. Bringing the water supply indoors to a sink, repairing doors and windows, tarring roofs and so on, work that is not covered by the improvement grant unless the five standard amenities are provided and the house brought up to the tolerable standard*'. This was also recognised by a group from Strathclyde University who looked at the possibility of developing a locally based improvement service similar to the ASSIST project in Glasgow but which never got off the ground. But this kind of thinking was to lead to 'Care and Repair' projects.

The Rural Forum report concluded that the reasons for the slow rate of improvement were complex, including inadequate financial support, administrative regulations that were not designed with rural conditions in mind, and the lack of innovation by local authorities. But it highlighted as a way forward the encouragement that Argyll and Bute had given to housing associations.

It also highlighted the poor or even non-existent information about the condition of the housing stock. It was not until 1991 that the first national house condition survey was carried out. Some local authorities conducted their own surveys as they were invited to do by the Government.

Demand and supply

The second major area that Rural Forum reviewed was that of the availability of housing – particularly to rent. In 1984 the main providers of rental accommodation were private landlords and local authorities. The report looked at the question of demand and supply.

Identifying rural housing needs from traditional sources was hard to assess. For example, using waiting lists was (and still is) no true measure. People did not put their names on waiting lists for many reasons: why put your name on a list if there are no houses being built, particularly if there are no houses in the settlement you want to live in? Anyway, the Council waiting list was likely only to be open to those whom the Council decided as being in need. Several categories of need were commonly excluded by Councils, including tenants of tied housing, those in winter lets, caravan dwellers and owner-occupiers. Some local authorities recognised the position. Banff and Buchan carried out a survey of its Mintlaw waiting list, and reported that a large number of applicants *were found to come from Deer where housing was unavailable; although the waiting list appeared to show a need in Mintlaw, and none in Deer, the survey revealed that the applicants preference would have been to stay in the Deer area.'*

Clearly, rural housing needs were there, but frequently rural needs were (and still are) less concentrated and obvious. As the report said *'Diffuse and hidden as rural needs may be, the evidence which exists unequivocally points to severe housing difficulties in many areas of rural and remote Scotland'*.

Low incomes were identified as the main cause of these needs. HIDB was quoted that low incomes *were 'by far the most important problem that affects the housing situation . . . low incomes are reflected in the inability of local people to compete with incomers; they are reflected in the difficulty of obtaining mortgages in the isolated areas; they are reflected in the generally small speculative building industry'*. Wages were relatively lower in rural Scotland, e.g. incomes in the Western Isles were thought to be less than 75% of those in major Scottish cities.

The rural housing problem therefore was not simply about being forgotten, but also about being hidden. The scale of demand was unknown; an example of the plight of the hidden people was shown in the extract from the report, itself extracted from an article written by Harper in the Press and Journal in 1982.

A 1983 survey showed that 313 people were living permanently in caravan and chalet accommodation in Skye and Lochalsh. 63% of them were local.

Some things have improved since 1984 and housing planning is one activity that has become more sophisticated, but there remains a question about the hidden demand in rural Scotland. It took some time for a better approach to measuring demand. It had not improved much by 1990 when, having been summoned to a meeting of a Council to explain why Scottish Homes was not investing in their area, your author explained that the investment plan was based upon two factors – homelessness demand as indicated by Council returns to the Scottish Office, and the number of BTS houses in the Council area. Since the Council had made no return for three years, it was assumed that there was no homelessness, and when asked about the number of BTS houses the Environmental Health Officer responded *'there are no BTS house in this District'*. Collapse of complaint; a return was quickly made and eventually a local house condition survey was carried out.

'In Skye you will find people living in old and dilapidated caravans – caravans neither wind nor water-tight; caravans well-nigh impossible to keep dry. You will find damp in the carpets, black mould on the walls and ceilings, and woodwork which crumbles to the touch. There are clusters of these old caravans on the edges of fields and waste ground all over the islands . . . Lucky tenants are hooked up to gas and electricity. May have no basic services at all. They carry their water from old taps. And the taps freeze in winter. If these caravans were houses they would have been condemned and pulled down long ago . . . These caravan-dwellers have fallen foul of Skye's acute shortage of proper council housing. Some have been on the list for years . . . One woman said that she and her husband had lived in their caravan for eight years . . . She says she had been waiting for a council house since 1974. She is not sure if she is even near the top of the waiting list . . .'

While the assessment of demand in 1984 was very difficult, the assessment of supply was equally difficult.

The easiest to calculate was **council housing** – and there analysis showed that Rural Scotland fared poorly compared to the rest of the country:

Council Housing	1971 (% total stock)	1981%
Scotland	54	54
Rural Scotland	38	
Orkney	17	22
Skye and Lochalsh	20	15
Western Isles	20	24
Kincardine and Deeside	26	25

The statistics once again hid a rural problem. Most of the council housing was in the larger towns, e.g. 22% of Orkney's population lived in council housing but outside of Kirkwall and Stromness the proportion was 7%. There were reasons for this, but not to do with demand. Difficulties in acquiring land, the lack of infrastructure, the additional costs of housebuilding in small developments away from larger centres, and the Government's financial regime which while it operated regional variations (allowing between 10% and 40% above the national average in more remote areas) did not recognise the additional costs away from the centres. All these still resonate today.

Council Housing

Local authority housing finance in 1984 occupied a large part of the report. Loan charges per dwelling were higher in remote and rural Scotland and with authorities having to rely more and more on rental income than government support, the more rural and remote authorities with small council stocks would be least able to increase income from rents. Thus the prediction that council building in rural Scotland would *'become ever rarer'*.

In addition, with local authorities becoming more dependent on rental income to finance any future programme, the smaller stock of council housing was forcing Councils to raise rents faster than elsewhere in Scotland. By 1983, the average council house rent in rural Scotland was 11% above the national average, and in remote Scotland it was 15%. And incomes were lower. The chances of developing a larger council house programme were slim.

The reduction in the share between 1971 and 1981 was partially caused by the introduction of the Right to Buy (RTB), and over the following years, the stock would be reduced considerably further, until Pressured Area status was introduced allowing Councils to opt out of RTB. (In 2014, legislation was passed to abolish RTB from 1 August 2016). Further, stock loss was not being replaced by new starts. There was a reduction of 49% of new starts in landward areas and small burghs between 1969 and 1973 (from 100 to 51). Meanwhile between April 1979 and September 1983, the Western Isles lost 10.4% of its council housing stock through RTB, Orkney, 9.3%, and Gordon 9.6%, compared to the national average of

3.7%. The highest RTB rates in the cities was in Edinburgh at 4.9%. Rural areas were being hit hardest by RTB.

Private rented

As for the private rented sector, understanding and measuring the scale of provision was even more complex. Rented accommodation in rural areas had been (and still is) predominately provided by landowners. In 1971 the proportion of households renting from private landlords was 25% in rural areas against the national average of 17%. The decline in the private sector at the national level was also happening in rural Scotland.

Quite a bit of the housing stock lay empty, and thus to a casual observer, it looked as if there was a surplus of accommodation. The reality was different. A Shelter survey for Gordon District Council highlighted a number of factors. Not all were habitable. Of the 1630 vacant dwellings, 503 (30%) were not habitable, although many could be modernized. Many were located close to settlements or bus routes, so could meet demand. Most were owned singly by private individuals. So why were they not being brought back into use? Uncertainties and lack of knowledge were a major part of the answer. Recent Rent Acts created uncertainty about security of tenure, while there were difficulties with finance for repairs and improvements. Owners appeared to be ignorant of the availability of improvement grants. And so the contribution that the private rented sector could make was not great.

Housing associations

This section of the report ended with the question – 'Is there a major role for housing associations in rural Scotland?'

The report was a very thorough document, and covered other key issues that remain rural housing issues today. These included Tied housing, Crofter housing, Holiday homes, Planning and Rural development. From the perspective of the housing association story, the most important was that of 'Special needs'. This is yet another area where our level of understanding of housing needs has become much more sophisticated. In

1984, the concern was for predominately about housing for elderly people – mainly sheltered housing – with the report highlighting the Highland Helpcall Scheme, providing a dispersed alarm system that enabled people to remain in their own home, but also mentioning that they were other needs that should be met, e.g. single person and those with disabilities. Provision against the then sheltered housing targets varied from 2% (in Wigton) to 149% (in Shetland) with an average of 30%. Again this was to prove an important role for housing associations.

1984 saw the case clearly made for increasing the housing association involvement in rural Scotland; the word 'increasing' is important – the ground work had already been established. The pioneers had already been at work.

CHAPTER THREE

1974

Opportunity Knocks

On the whole Governments do not pioneer new ideas using legislation. They respond to demand even if they take the credit for being innovative. They may respond to pressure from formal inquiries which they set up (such as the Royal Commission that reported in 1917); to pressure from MPs who in turn are pressured by constituents; and to pressure from good research and lobby groups. It was a mixture of all three that led to the two 1974 Housing Acts that brought a change in the opportunities for housing associations. The first of these – purely for Scotland – was designed to improve the quality of the older housing stock and particularly tenements. Indeed in some quarters it was dubbed 'the Glasgow Act', since much of its provisions were designed to drive the improvement of Glasgow tenements, following the experiences of the city. It concentrated on Housing Action Areas, but also reviewed the grant arrangements for improving sub tolerable housing.

The other legislation was the Housing Act 1974. This provided a new regime for housing associations for the whole of Great Britain. The ability of housing associations to deliver more homes was clearly being constrained by the funding (or lack of funding) regime. Campaigns by Shelter and the National Federation of Housing Associations led to a Housing Bill being promoted first by the Heath Government in 1973. This bill however fell with the Tory Government, but was picked up almost word for word by the incoming Labour administration. So it had the full cross party support, a position that was to be essential in the years ahead. The new regime would provide funding in the form of Housing Association Grant (HAG) and public sector loans, providing the association was registered with the Housing Corporation and subject to its regulation.

The Housing Corporation had been set up in 1964 with a Scottish

'Regional' Office in Edinburgh. Its first ten years it had been concerned predominately with co-ownership and cost rent housing in the central belt. Its new challenge was to deal with tenements. A Glasgow office was set up in 1974 to deal firstly with that city. The approach adopted was that of developing and supporting new local housing associations by working with local residents to create their own community based association and then to help to buy tenement flats and improve them with bathrooms and good repair work using grants from the Housing Corporation. Although Glasgow was the main target, the office was allowed to consider other urban areas. Very soon the Director of Housing for the new Argyll and Bute Council, Bob Couper, arrived at the office door. Local authorities had been reorganised also in 1974. The old councils had been swept away, with a two tier structure of Regions and Districts. The key function of the Districts was housing and the newly appointed Directors were taking a fresh look at the challenges they faced. Many of the old county councils had simply built houses from time to time and a number did not have a proper housing department.

Bob Couper was one of the new breed. He was to play a key role in the 1984 Rural Forum report. He was looking strategically at the housing needs of the district and not just at providing council housing. He had identified Rothesay as a major issue. Fyne Homes based in Rothesay, and covering much of Argyll, describes the situation: *'In 1974, Argyll and Bute District Council as successor to Rothesay Town and Bute County Council carried out a housing survey on the Island of Bute. In Rothesay the capital of this island, which had been a Mecca for countless holiday makers from the West of Scotland, and immortalised in song and folklore, described as the best remaining example of a Victorian/Edwardian seaside town, home to the largest continuous Outstanding Conservation Area out with Edinburgh's New Town – more than half the houses in the town centre were Below the Tolerable Standard (BTS) and half of these lacked even basic standard amenities. In the latter half of the 20th century over 300 homes didn't have an inside lavatory'*

So the Housing Corporation was asked to come down to Rothesay. An urban problem (tenements) in a rural setting allowed the Corporation to support the Council initiative. Fyne Homes explains what happened next: *'Following the largest public meeting seen on the Island, Isle of Bute Housing Association (later Bute Housing Association) was formed as the first Community Based Housing Association outwith the Glasgow conurbation to tackle the problem. Over the next decade through a Housing Action Area programme of rehabilitation, demolition and new build 700 quality affordable new homes were provided in the historic heart of the town and in Port Bannatyne and Kingarth.*

Rothesay Conservation Area is unique in that it is made up almost entirely of working class tenements, some listed in their own right, and through the association new life was breathed into these tenement areas, including two impressive Georgian tenements predating Rothesay's holiday resort fame and a product of its previous little known past as a centre for the nascent cotton industry with its water powered mills, sadly none of which now survive, although the mill lade is soon to be transformed into a major feature of a heritage trail'.

Early days

The Isle of Bute Housing Association was not the first association in Bute nor in Argyll. A number of housing associations had pre-dated the 1974 Act. William Woodhouse Strain was one of the first in Scotland. And along with Bute Housing Association (and others) it has become Fyne Homes.

William Woodhouse Strain was inaugurated on 28 February 1961. Indeed its history goes back even further. In 1936 William Woodhouse Strain, a Glasgow Solicitor bequeathed land and buildings at Port Bannatyne in Trust to Bute County Council. Woodhouse Strain was concerned at the plight of farm workers who were dependent on tied housing and when they lost their jobs or retired found themselves homeless. The bequest was to be used to house those who found themselves in these circumstances.

Times fortunately moved on and by the 1960s this was not such an issue. The buildings, having outlived their usefulness, had been demolished and the Council decided to seek Court of Session Approval to alter the terms of the bequest to allow them to build houses on the site by forming the Trust into a Housing Association. This was granted, provided lettings were prioritised in accordance with the original bequest, and the newly formed William Woodhouse Strain Housing Association built eight flats on the site at Shore Road Port Bannatyne.

At the other side of Scotland, other people were considering how housing associations could solve the poor housing conditions in the very small fishing village of Auchmithie in Angus. Angus Housing Association traces its history back to 1970 when a factor, a lawyer and an accountant decide to use the relatively new idea of a housing association to save the village. This was not simply about providing housing, but regeneration – something that will feature in much of the work of rural associations.

The reasons why housing associations have developed in rural areas are quite varied, as are the ways in which they were started.

Shetland was one of the early areas. With the growth of the oil industry in the North Sea demand for housing in Shetland was at a premium. In the 1970s Sumburgh Airport suddenly grew from a small island ex-military base with a few scheduled services to being the fastest growing airport in the UK and a major helicopter base. Housing for the operational staff was very poor. Scottish Airports Housing Association (SAHA) was created in 1974 to provide accommodation for Civil Aviation Authority, Bristow Helicopters and British Airways staff. A year later, with the development of Sullom Voe, Hjaltland Housing Association was created to house workers at the oil terminal, in particular middle managers. The association worked closely with the Council to meet local needs. The housing association expertise came from Link Housing Association in Edinburgh and from Bob Soper, an Edinburgh based quantity surveyor who acted as Secretary to both Committees. The two associations merged under the Hjaltland name in 1980 since it was felt that Shetland was too small for two associations. The combined organisations could then afford to be locally run.

Gordon Mitchell was for many years the chair of Hjaltland and managing pilot at Bristow. Why did he get involved? *'I was an association tenant and had become concerned about the poor standard of the SAHA properties at that time. Even though these had been new properties they had been built to much lower standards. There were issues with ongoing snagging problems as well as poor construction. Many tenants suffered from leaking properties, insufficient heating and insufficient electrical wiring. At that time Link management only came up once a month and this was not felt to be enough to get issues resolved'.* Gordon became involved to ensure better management of the houses. He became chairman of the tenants committee to liaise with Link and then after this was taken onto Hjaltland committee. And he stayed. One of the lessons from the Hjaltland story was to be the importance of local control, of local management and a continuing strong local partnership with the local authority.

Alongside the development of local based rural associations that provided for a variety of housing needs, there were associations which were very active in providing accommodation for particular groups. For years they have been known as Special Needs associations, usually with a head office in the central belt. Hanover (Scotland) is one of those – building sheltered housing with warden support across the country. It had started as a regional division of a UK wide organisation and by 1978 had become a Scottish based association. Before 'independence' its first development in Scotland had been in rural locations – and these were the first sheltered housing in the country. The group of associations like Hanover operating across the country were known as 'nationals' and their growth continued alongside the development of more local associations. This partly reflected a funding policy by the Housing Corporation which implied that only specialist associations had the skills and expertise to provide accommodation for elderly and disabled people. It also reflected the funding priorities agreed with the Secretary of State for Scotland of area renewal and special needs. In the early years after 1974, the area renewal work had been concentrated in urban private sector tenement rented housing. Thus Rothesay fitted the policy. The earliest Housing Corporation rural investment was through special needs associations, but this was to slowly change. In the early days after 1974 the Housing Corporation did not have a monopoly of funding. Associations could obtain grants and loans from local authorities through a programme centrally controlled by the Scottish Development Department and the majority of these funds went to rural areas.

Another of the early pioneers was Albyn Housing Society established in 1973 as the legislation to create the 1974 Housing Act was passing through Parliament. Based in Invergordon, this was promoted by the Adam Housing Society in Edinburgh, with a local committee but serviced from Edinburgh. It was to provide general needs housing with a Highland wide commitment. It arrived at the right time. Money was about to be available for development on an unprecedented scale, but as usual there was to be price. It was called Registration and Supervision.

The Housing Corporation that was given the responsibility of turning a group of disparate housing organisations into a major force in the provision of affordable housing arrived with the strong political support. And one of the first things that the Corporation wanted to do was to clarify that those who were to benefit through contracts (architects, surveyors,

Hanover Scotland – a national association with rural commitment

Established in 1963 in Surrey, Hanover Housing Association was the first UK organisation dedicated to providing purpose-built, rented accommodation for older people. Two of its early developments were at Scone and Drymen, the first sheltered accommodation provided by a housing association in Scotland. After the Association opened a Scottish Regional Office in 1976, a fast-growing development portfolio led to the setting up of a Scottish Advisory Committee whose goal was independence. This was encouraged by the Housing Corporation and in October 1978 Hanover (Scotland) Housing Association Ltd, as a totally separate entity under the chairmanship of former Secretary of State for Scotland, Michael Noble, Lord Glenkinglas.

From the start Hanover explored new forms of housing and built sheltered housing schemes in both urban and mainland rural Scotland. It undertook its first conversions of existing buildings in Bathgate and Keith; investigated new types of tenure such as shared equity; and signed its first agency agreement, to develop accommodation on behalf of a small Borders housing association.

Sheltered housing managers, initially known as wardens, are the lynchpin in delivering services. The first annual report summed up what was expected of a sheltered housing manager: 'Their role requires a subtle combination of sensitivity and tact in certain circumstances and level headedness and even firmness in other situations.'

Although still most closely associated with new housing, over the past thirty years Hanover has created homes from redundant buildings, remodelled or replaced its own properties for new uses and partnered other organisations in the renewal of run-down localities. In rural areas, from Dalbeattie to Elgin, where land was scarce, Hanover awarded design and build contracts to local builders in return for releasing land. It may have been the first housing association in Scotland to use design and build, in its Auchinairn Road development in Bishopbriggs.

From the start Hanover participated as a partner in urban renewal, and this was extended to rural areas. Hanover established a new organisation - Hanover (Caol) Housing Association – to take over, demolish and rebuild an estate of structurally unsound, pre-cast concrete system-built houses owned by Lochaber District Council. In 1990/91 Hanover worked closely with the Council and the tenants' committee in designing the new development of fifty family homes outside Fort William.

In the late 1990s, under the Empty Homes Initiative, Hanover moved into refurbishing existing buildings. It created six homes for families and independent, older people in a former surgery in Buckie. It also adapted its own properties for new purposes. In 2003, for example, three, difficult-to-let, sheltered flats in Lumsden, Aberdeenshire provided living space for sculptors at the neighbouring workshop of the Scottish Sculpture Trust. Since the 1990s when managers no longer had to 'live above the shop', their flats have been turned into additional accommodation for residents.

Despite tight budget constraints, Hanover aimed to produce architecture that was not only fit for purpose but also added to the local townscape. It was awarded its first Saltire Award in 1980 for Hanover Court, Stonehaven which also won a Civic Trust commendation two years later. In all, Hanover has won eleven such awards. A particularly challenging award-winner in 2003 was Murdoch Nisbet Court, ten amenity flats for older people and two family homes, within the historic centre of Newmilns, Ayrshire. Flexibility and sustainability are built into design in a way that was unheard of thirty years ago. Accommodation is based largely on two bedrooms so that it can be switched from sheltered to amenity or even family housing. Sustainability has led to significant improvements in thermal insulation and the installation of solar panels and biomass heating systems.

lawyers, etc) would not play a controlling role on the association's governing body. Registered housing associations were to be run by volunteers. In addition, wherever possible, associations should have their own staff. Thus, over a period of time, the rural based housing associations that were run from the central belt – like Albyn and Hjaltland – had both voluntary-only committee members, and their own staff located in the rural area.

Planned Growth

In the first twelve years of Housing Corporation funding, rural areas (using the District Council area definition) had accounted for only 10% of the houses funded (3% of rehabilitation; 23% of new build). By the year 1985-86 there had been a significant change. Rural areas now accounted for 20% (12% of rehabilitation; 42% of new build). This was as a result of the funding priorities being reviewed in 1983. New build was no longer restricted to sheltered housing and diversification into smaller settlements was being encouraged. Rehabilitation was no longer confined to tenements. The objective was to improve the housing stock and to regenerate local communities. And a larger number of associations were operating in 'rural' areas – twenty-three out of the eighty-six associations being supported within Scotland. Of these a number were 'local associations' being promoted or encouraged to develop by the Corporation's investment strategy.

The characteristics of these new associations included:

- Concerned with a limited geographical area
- Membership (shareholding) limited to local residents
- Locally based staff
- Work in close liaison with local authorities
- Multi-purpose, capable of undertaking rehabilitation, new building, special needs and low cost home ownership
- Future not simply in housing terms, but as local institutions involved in the regeneration of their area

There were strong similarities to the community based housing associations working in urban area renewal. The first of the new associations was Buidheann Tigheadas Loch Aillse agus an Eilein Sgitheanaich (Lochalsh and Skye Housing Association). Following agreement with Skye and Lochalsh District Council about the housing needs in the district, and with the active leadership of Andrew Leslie from the Edinburgh office of the Housing Corporation, a group of local people met at the Royal Hotel, Portree, on 21 March 1983 to inaugurate the association. Andrew Leslie and his colleague Rob Milne provided initial induction training and support. However, the fledgling association needed to have more local secretarial and development support to get its first housing development out of the ground. The Skye and Lochalsh Council of Voluntary Service fulfilled this role, in the person of its secretary, Pat Gordon, with back up from the Housing Corporation until the association had generated sufficient headway to appoint its first (and so far its only) full time director. Lachie MacDonald started in 1986, and it was maybe no coincidence that Lachie had previously been the Director of Central Govan Housing Association which was the first community based housing association.

This pattern was followed for a number of associations: agreement between the District Council and the Housing Corporation on the local needs that could be met by a housing association; working with a group of volunteers or with a local organisation, e.g. Community Council;

training of the new committee; providing support in the early days through providing a grant to hire staff or buy services from another association. Associations were unable to do much in the way of development work without having some staff, but since associations were funded through development allowances, there was little opportunity for them to hire staff until some development had been undertaken. Catch 22? But where a strategy had been agreed with a local authority, the Housing Corporation was able to give start up grant, or to arrange some from the local authority. In some cases, the Highlands and Islands Development Board (now Highlands and Islands Enterprise) gave a grant on the basis that the association was creating local jobs.

In some District Council areas there was no need to promote a 'local' association. There were associations already operating in some areas and often obtaining grant through the local authority. Associations such as Eildon in the Borders and Albyn in Invernesshire. Rather than promoting new associations the Housing Corporation talked to them about becoming the local or regional associations, with much of the characteristics of the new ones.

By 1986, two years after the Rural Forum report, the Housing Corporation, with the support of a rural working party of the Scottish Federation of Housing Associations, reviewed the rural dimension of its Investment Strategy. By this time, it was clear that future investment, and in many ways the future direction of the housing association movement itself, needed a more sophisticated approach. Other organisations were also developing rural housing initiatives. Shelter launched its Rural Housing Initiative, which focused initially on bringing empty homes back into use. The project officer was Di Alexander. A joint project between Shelter and Age Concern on Care and Repair was to lead to other important roles for housing associations.

Rural housing was coming up the agenda. With the growing number of associations in rural areas, the Scottish Federation of Housing Associations created a rural forum for mutual support and lobbying – RIHAF, the Rural and Islands Housing Associations Forum.

The Housing Corporation's review gave rural a high priority, with a number of areas being 'Designated' as areas for development. These would be targeted for resources over a number of years with the objective of stabilising the population as part of a programme of rural regeneration.

The plan was that these would be partnership areas with local authorities, the HIDB and where appropriate the Scottish Development Area (SDA) to ensure that economic development and housing development went hand in hand. Settlements would be small; there had to be an overall plan covering infrastructure and economic development. Within these Designated Areas, associations would be funded to rehabilitate the houses in the poorest condition and provide replacement homes for rent and low cost home ownership (including providing an agency service to other owners) including for special needs.

Examples of early housing association experiences that contributed to the strategic thinking in 1986

- **Isle of Bute Housing Association** now owned over 400 homes. Early in its development, the Association realised that the tenements it aimed to rehabilitate contained a significant number of second homes which contributed to the economic base of the community. Simply to do away with these flats would be detrimental to the local economy, but at the same time the accommodation was in an unsatisfactory condition. With the support of HIDB, the Association helped to set up a community business which provided locally-owned self-catering accommodation, properly integrated into the tenement improvement programme.

- In Wigtown, within the Machar Development Area, **Loreburn Housing Association** had been working with the local development organisation, identifying small scale housing schemes which are required to ensure accommodation for those currently employed and thus protecting the economic base.

- In Deeside, **Castlehill Housing Association** built eight sheltered houses in the village of Finzean. The houses were allocated to local residents, thus freeing up family housing. By its location, the sheltered housing protected the future of the local shop/post office, and the bus stop was at the door.

- Nearby, **Langstane Housing Association** converted storage stables into a scheme of two rehabilitated and two new build homes as well as four workshops. The Housing Corporation funded the houses, the SDA the workshops, and Banff and Buchan District Council built a car park to enable visitors to stop at the local shop, pub and workshops on the way to Fyvie Castle.

Much of this was built upon existing housing association activity; upon the experience of those organisations that had been developing over the last eight years. The map shows the extent of local and regional associations in 1988. The new Investment Strategy was designed to expand the programme. But before it could be fully implemented, there were big changes coming. The Housing Corporation was about to disappear.

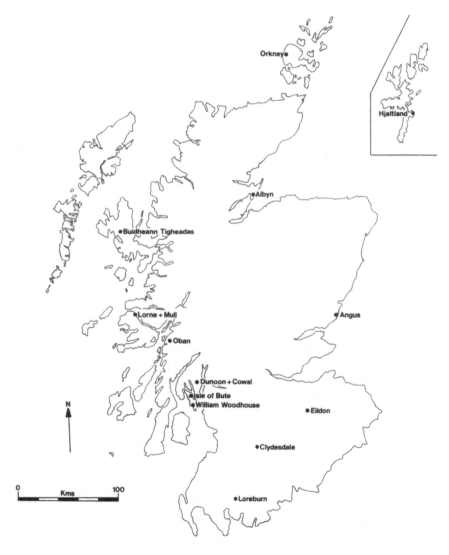

Map of locally based rural HAs in 1988.

CHAPTER FOUR

1990

A Rural Housing Policy

The growth of housing associations in Scotland brought with it a tension within the Housing Corporation. Both rural and urban programmes were growing fast. With the prospect of devolution in the Scotland Act of 1978, the Corporation had set up what became known as the 'Housing Corporation in Scotland' (HCiS) with significant delegated authority under the guidance of a Scottish Committee chaired (from 1982) by John Richards, one of Scotland's leading architects. The funding came from the Scottish Office allocation, but as the Corporation was a Great Britain organisation, there remained a certain amount of control from London. The policies of the two parts of the Corporation did not always coincide; indeed there were considerable differences in their approach, with Scotland adopting the 'Scottish solutions to Scottish problems' (to quote Donald Dewar after the Scottish Parliament came into being).

By the late 1980s, HCiS was investing a very large proportion of the Scottish housing budget in housing associations. Conservative Ministers, Secretary of State Malcolm Rifkind and Housing Minister Michael Ancrum, were pursuing a policy of reducing council owned housing through Right to Buy and transfer of public sector estates to housing associations. As early as 1979, Douglas Niven had called for a 'Scottish Housing Board'. This was an idea whose time was about to come. The Scottish Special Housing Association (SSHA) was a state sponsored housing agency that had been created in 1937 to help with regeneration and overspill. It had been subject of a regular review, and in the introduction to the published review, Rifkind wrote: *'I have been conscious of the need to look at the role of SSHA in the wider context of overall housing activity in Scotland, over which government (i.e. Scotland) exercises control. While each of the main bodies concerned has its own distinctive approach and contribution to make to housing needs, there is common ground and some overlap in their activities.'* HCiS was not immediately convinced, concerned that the larger organisation could create a stranglehold over the kind of relationship that HCiS had with the developing housing associations. But it was a rural housing association opening that changed the minds of the Scottish based members of the Scottish Committee.

The Chairman of the Housing Corporation, Sir Hugh Cubitt, had been invited in May 1985 to open Lochalsh and Skye Housing Association's first property at Lephin Park, Glendale, and to hand the keys of the first house over to Mrs. Marion Morrison. Sir Hugh flew into the then Broadford airport. He was recovering from a broken leg but had insisted in undertaking the opening. Housing Conveners from the surrounding District Councils were in attendance and the Housing Corporation was providing some hospitality in the evening. Over dinner, Sir Hugh asked about the cost of the houses. For that time they were relatively expensive, as one would expect building four houses predominately for elderly people in a relatively remote location. The comment from London was 'would it not have been cheaper to move the elderly people to a house in Inverness where the capital costs would have been significantly less?' The Scottish response was twofold. First, that if the capital cost was the criteria, then the Housing Corporation should stop building in London which had the highest costs in the UK. Secondly, and afterwards, the Scottish Committee members said to Ministers that separation from London could be in the interests of the housing association sector in Scotland, since London really did not fully understand the nature of Scotland. And thus the rural contribution to the merger with SSHA which created Scottish Homes.

Maybe it was not a coincidence that the place which sparked the debate was Glendale. It has a special

Glendale development.
Photo from Lochalsh and Skye HA

place in the history of Gàidhealtachd, and in the fight for decent rural housing. In 1883, the landlord refused the crofters permission to collect wood from the shore for heating, while they had to use straw to thatch their houses as they were forbidden to cut the marram grass and rushes. The common grazing ground had also been denied. Direct action was the crofters' only possibility and they began grazing their cattle on what had been common ground despite courts orders for their removal. The police were called in January but the crofters refused to budge, and the navy gunboat HMS *Jackal* with a government official on board tried negotiations. Five crofters agreed to stand in a token trial. Sentenced to two months in jail, they became the Glendale Martyrs. The government response also included setting up the Napier Commission to investigate crofters' grievances which ultimately led to the Crofters Act of 1886. Glendale has a more than one place in Scotland's community housing history.

Nor was the contribution of rural housing associations to be forgotten when Scottish Homes was born on 1 April 1989 as the national housing agency. The new body quickly moved to build upon the strategic work that had been established by HCiS and set up a Rural Committee under the chairmanship of board member Heather Sheerin. Heather was a business woman in Inverness. She was also a member of Albyn Housing Society and therefore came with an understanding and experience of rural housing. With the Regional Director North (your author, who had secured a policy remit outwith the central policy unit) as the committee's officer, the Committee set about producing a Rural Policy. Other Scottish Homes staff, particularly Coinneach Maclean (District manager for Highlands and Islands) and Jim Walsh (District Manager Lothian and Borders) became part of the team, with Mark Shucksmith (then of Aberdeen University) as adviser. The team was also encouraged by the support of the Highlands and Islands Development Board. One the first phone calls received when Scottish Homes began was from the Board's Chairman Sir Robert Cowan who said '*We need to talk, we can do very little about economic development without housing*'.

Scottish Homes was a different kind of organisation to HCiS. For a start, housing associations were only part of its responsibilities. It was to be concerned with the whole housing system, including home ownership and the private rented sector. It also inherited the entire housing stock of SSHA. It was to promote a consumerist approach to housing. Demand

Heather Sheerin
Photo from Scottish Homes collection

was as important as needs. To achieve this, Scottish Homes had wide powers and was tasked with both leading on the Government's desire for market solutions and intervening in the many areas of multiple deprivation, particularly in urban Scotland. Ideally the Government wanted both at the same time. And that meant applying market solutions wherever possible to the public sector, including the ex-SSHA stock which was spread across the country. But this also meant making a major impact on local authority owned housing, for which Scottish Homes was seen by many people, particularly on the left, as a politically motivated organisation. In some ways that perception, reinforced by the chairman, Sir James Mellon, taking a high profile market orientated approach, overshadowed the benefits and achievements of looking at housing 'in the round'. One of Sir James' favourite sayings reflected the change in the kind of organisation. Referring to housing associations, we warned that Scottish Homes 'was not a one club golfer'. Scottish Homes was not necessarily welcomed in every quarter.

Scottish Homes therefore had a particular approach to policy development. The whole system had to be looked at and not just one sector. Policy making was to involve research and consultation. Research included undertaking the first national house condition survey, socio-economic analysis, technical investigations and consumer information. Policy was to be based on evidence, on market analysis and consultation. As far as a rural policy was concerned this was good news – and the wider powers that Scottish Homes was given would enable a range of funding and other support.

The policy review began with a consultative paper *The Rural Housing Challenge* that was discussed at a series of consultation events from Kirkwall to Shotts. Research on the effectiveness and future role of housing associations that had been started under HCiS was fed into an information gathering process and a series of Local Study Areas was commissioned. Arguments were set out on why rural housing required a different approach with analysis on population changes, house condition, supply constraints, access to affordable housing, market imbalances and the quality of data available. In addition, the question of the rural definition was raised once again.

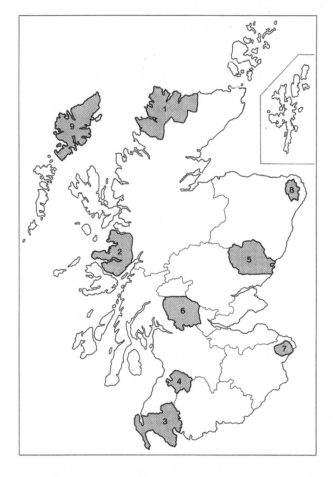

Map of local study areas from the Scottish Homes Rural Policy.

1. North West Sutherland.

2. Ardnamurchan and South Lochaber.

3. Wigtownshire.

4. South Cumnock and Doon Valley.

5. Forfar, Brechin and Angus Glens.

6. West Stirlingshire

7. Duns and Chirnside.

8. Central Buchan.

9. Lewis and Harris.

All of this was set against a set of principles that Scottish Homes would adopt:

Scottish Homes Principles

- Working in partnership – 'ultimately, the rural housing challenge is best addressed by rural people themselves, with whatever support Scottish Homes and others can provide'
- A new rural approach should be developed, rather than merely revamping an in appropriate urban response
- An approach should be developed which can be tailored to local circumstances
- A rural policy should be developed which contributes towards broad rural housing objectives, as well as more specific housing goals.
- A policy should be developed of supporting rural development through working with rural communities
- Careful consideration should be given to affordability as well as to development costs
- Investment and resources should be directed to where they are most needed and to those who need them

The resultant policy was given a high profile launch at conference in Aviemore in September 1990 with Princess Anne giving a keynote speech, and the Housing Minister, Lord James Douglas Hamilton, launching the policy. Rural housing was in the news.

Four key issues in rural housing were identified, similar to the Rural Forum key issues, with the addition of participation:

- Increasing housing supply
- Improving house condition
- The cost of and access to rural housing
- Resident participation and involvement as part of community development

While the policy document was called 'The Role of Scottish Homes in Rural Scotland', it set out proposals that would have an impact on the way housing associations (and others) were to develop if they wanted support from Scottish Homes. For the Agency it identified three enabling roles:

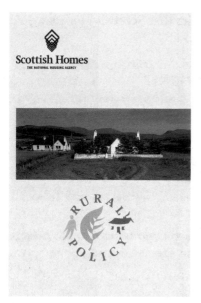

The cover of the Scottish Homes Rural Policy.

- Collecting and disseminating information
- Stimulating the provision of housing 'by private sector bodies (including housing associations) working in partnership with local authorities and others'
- Providing grants to those private sector organisations.

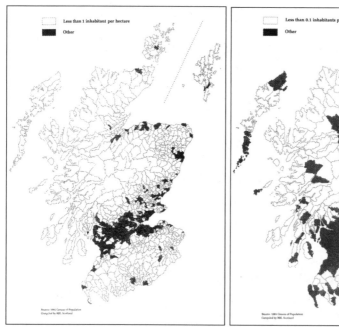

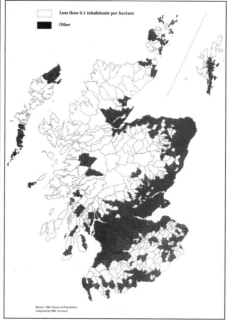

Left:
Parishes with less than 1 inhabitant per hectare from the Scottish Homes Rural Policy.

Right:
Parishes with less than 0.1 inhabitant per hectare from the Scottish Homes Rural Policy.

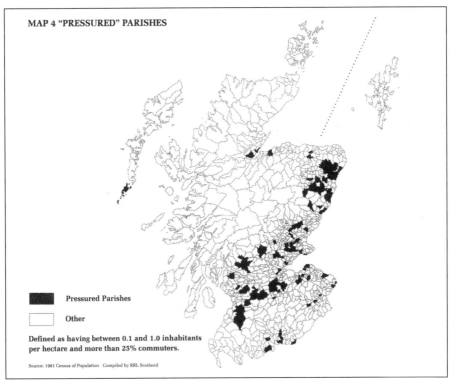

MAP 4 "PRESSURED" PARISHES

Pressured Parishes

Other

Defined as having between 0.1 and 1.0 inhabitants
per hectare and more than 25% commuters.

Source: 1981 Census of Population   Compiled by RRL Scotland

'Pressured parishes' from the Scottish Homes Rural Policy.

Collecting and disseminating information

The first of these involved a new working definition of rural Scotland;
developed for Scottish Homes by Mark Shucksmith. This was to be more
fine-grained than any previous definition. It would be parish based, with
rural parishes being all those with less than one person per hectare, remote
with less than 0.1 person per hectare, and the identification of 'pressured'
parishes where more than 25% of the population were commuters. It
solved the problem of Arran being urban and Inverness rural. But it meant
that places like Kelso, Brechin, Thurso and even Rothesay were no longer
rural. The answer to their needs was that Scottish Homes was also
developing a Smaller Urban Renewal Initiative (SURI) intended to ensure
that urban settlements in rural areas would have their housing needs
considered alongside other priorities. It also recognised that different

solutions were required in different places. The analysis that accompanied the definition showed the differences between the new definition and one based on District Councils (1981 census figures):

Percentage in category	DC Definition	SH Rural	SH Remote	Scotland Total
Households	27.4	17.0	4.0	100.0
Tenure Owner occupied and crofter	61.4	61.2	72.7	44.8
Public (incl. HAs)	38.6	37.3	27.0	54.6
HAs	N/A	0.6	0.3	1.6
Stock condition – without exclusive use of amenities	N/A	3.3	5.1	2.8
Population age profile (from General Register office)				
• Under 5	6.3	6.3	6.3	6.1
• 5–64	77.9	78.3	77.7	82.4
• Over 65	15.8	15.4	16.0	11.5

Although the differences were not dramatic, it threw up sufficient evidence that both rural and remote areas had well above average poor condition; considerably less than average housing association activity; and above average elderly people, many of whom were living in some of the poorest housing.

Stimulating private sector bodies

For the purposes of the policy report housing associations were firmly seen as private sector organisations. They had always been neither true public nor for profit private. They were not for profit bodies and had also been termed the 'Voluntary Housing Movement' since the governing boards were all volunteers. This did not mean that they could not make a surplus or profit on their activities, but they were not able to distribute that surplus. But in the political language of the time, they had to be seen as 'not public sector' and therefore had to be 'private sector'. But this would enable them to play a major and increasing role. The policy set out an expansion of housing association activity, both in meeting the needs of associations' traditional client groups and in diversifying and broadening their activities. New associations were to be encouraged. In some ways this was a confirmation of the HCiS plan for housing associations. But there were to be further opportunities, given the new powers of Scottish Homes. Care in the Community was to be encouraged. Associations were to be involved with rural low cost home ownership (LCHO) schemes, including shared ownership. And a whole new idea in which associations would come to play a major part was proposed – Local Housing Agencies (LHAs).

One of the main concerns raised during the consultation period had been how support could be given to 'relevant organisations' for securing the delivery of services and advice to housing providers consumers operating in rural areas. LHA was to be a label rather than a structure; these 'relevant organisations' could be community businesses, housing associations, housing trusts, or bodies connected to Local Enterprise Companies which were part of the HIDB or Scottish Enterprise networks. It was envisaged that the 'agency' could act on behalf of both Scottish Homes and local authorities (and indeed others) by providing a more local service than was possible within existing organisational structures. The preference was for housing associations to take on the role. With a few exceptions this is what happened. The exceptions came in the form of the Rural Forum (now Rural Housing Scotland), and two key trusts – Highlands Small Community Housing Trust and Dumfries and Galloway Housing Trust. The economic companies did not take on the role, although joint ventures with the economic development bodies were envisaged and have proved to be effective.

The LHA model was designed to encourage associations to undertake a number of possible services, depending on local needs e.g.:

- Housing advice and promoting rural rehabilitation including through Care and Repair schemes.
- Providing a development and management function for smaller associations.
- Helping with market analysis.

- Promoting and supporting individual self-builders
- Land assembly
- Receiving and managing housing transferred by other landlords (e.g. large land owners or local authorities)

Some of these were to work well, others not so well. The LHA label itself disappeared quite quickly. But the principle of a housing association providing not just rented housing but housing services to a community was now firmly established.

Providing grants

In supporting housing associations Scottish Homes aimed to provide more houses for a given amount of public resource. Private finance was to become a feature. No longer would there be total finance from public sources. However, there was a recognition that there was a need for flexibility within the Housing Association Grant (HAG) regime to consider higher levels of grant where it could be demonstrated that there were justifiable costs of site acquisition, servicing and procurement in rural areas.

The policy also introduced some new funding opportunities. As could be expected, given the overall priorities, these were mainly on the LCHO front, including Improvement for Sale (IFS) to upgrade sub tolerable housing and bring into use empty housing, and shared ownership. For the latter, there was a suggestion that work would be done to find ways to ensure that the houses remained available for priority groups for resale. One area for development was that of Care and Repair which had been successfully piloted by Shelter and Age Concern.

The intention was that there should be a wide menu of options which could be used to meet housing needs, and a recognition that what was needed in rural areas was small bespoke developments that made a social and, where appropriate, an economic contribution. These small scale developments would be in contrast to the large urban regeneration programmes required in the central belt. As someone put it: 'rural Scotland needs hand crafted pies compared to the sausage machine required in Glasgow's peripheral estates'.

One grant typified this approach. Scottish Homes LCHO powers enabled the creation of a grant to individuals which was modelled on the grants that had been available for years for crofters through the Crofters Grant and Loan scheme. The argument was that the second and third sons and daughters of the croft could get a piece of ground from their crofter parent or senior sibling (whoever was the crofter), but could not get any assistance with building costs. So the RHOG grant (Rural Home Ownership Grant) was created. Perhaps a bureaucratic nightmare, but a grant mechanism designed for specific purposes. And an ideal candidate for being managed by LHAs.

Obtaining and servicing land for development was, as usual, highlighted as a problem. Included in the discussions about land was the issue of retaining housing for local people or of preventing publicly funded developments from becoming second homes. However, the most pressing issue related to obtaining land for social housing, particularly for housing associations. One option, and the most expensive one, was to pay additional HAG reflecting higher market values where competition for land was at its greatest. There were two other proposals. First, that land in public ownership should be sold to housing associations at less than market value. Second, in areas with particular supply side constraints and pressures, local planning policies might make it clear that certain sites could be released which would ensure provision of low cost housing for local needs additional to the provision made in the plan for general housing demand. Secure arrangements would have to be in place which would restrict tenure or occupancy. And the report noted that the land tenure system was the subject of a major review by the Scottish Land Commission.

A longer term agenda was also identified, including reviewing the impact of 'Right to Buy' in rural areas; arrangements to mobilise private finance; tackling more directly the problem of tenant and community participation in remote and sparse rural areas; highlighting quality and design issues in low cost housing with continuing work on typology of rural areas and the development of indicators to identify priority client groups.

The Scottish Homes Rural Policy was seen by many as a significant step forward. It provided rural housing associations with a menu for the future. What about its implementation?

CHAPTER FIVE

1990

Change and delivery

The 1990s saw an explosion of rural policy statements, framework documents, reorganisations and partnerships. And names. All would have an impact on the way housing associations were to operate.

The Highlands and Islands Development Board had metamorphosed into Highlands and Islands Enterprise (HIE) in 1991 (and the Scottish Development Agency had become Scottish Enterprise). A year later the Scottish Office Rural Framework set out a new coordinated way of tackling rural problems. In 1993, Scottish Homes, barely four years old, reorganised from multipurpose regions to a functional structure, and the rural policy was absorbed into the central policy team. The Scottish office published the first rural White Paper *Rural Scotland: People, Prosperity and Partnership*, quickly followed by a Rural Partnership fund and the setting up of a series of Local Rural Partnerships

However, the three biggest changes were still to come. All were political and impacted on governance. First, in 1996, the local government structure which had served since 1975 was reorganised. The two tier structure with Regions and District Councils was swept away and replaced with thirty-two single tier authorities. Some of the Councils, particularly in rural areas, covered a very large area. Highland Council was (and still is) responsible for the largest local government area in the UK with a land mass larger than Belgium and a population of 232,000 in 2010. While the new Councils were settling down, 1997 saw a change of Government and new policies, with the Labour Party committed to Scottish devolution. And in 1999, the Scottish Parliament met for the first time since 1707. It was a decade of huge change.

At the same time, new or better quality information was becoming available to help with the planning process. In 1993, the first Scottish House Condition Survey (SHCS) was published using data collected in 1991.The rural information was analysed on the broadest of the Scottish

Homes Rural Policy definitions, giving a rural/urban split of 17:83. It did not produce many surprises. It reinforced the poor quality of the housing stock, highlighted the difference in the pre-1919 stock, with (36% in rural compared to 18% in urban) and in the post 1960 stock (32% rural, 40% urban). Of course the SHCS only dealt with permanent homes and did not take into account temporary homes like caravans (estimated at 4000 households in 1993) and therefore could not fully represent the housing conditions that rural Scots were living in.

With apologies to the late Ewan Bain – this cartoon first emerged as Angus Og's comment on the 1991 census. It was amended and used as part of the presentations on the first Scottish House Condition Survey.

Other players were also impacting on rural housing. Shelter continued with its empty homes initiative. A new development was Rural Forum's Rural Housing Service. With funding from Scottish Homes' HomePoint and Skye and Lochalsh District Council, Di Alexander, who had become the Forum's Rural Housing Officer, launched the concept of Personal Housing Plans which fitted alongside the menu of support to individuals. He also developed community housing needs surveys enabling local communities to be responsible for their own market analysis, and thus being able to make their case for affordable housing investment in their area. The communities did not only look for support to undertake market analysis, but also to be 'enabled' to deal with the paper work, bureaucracy and processes that inevitably form part of creating a housing development. The role of 'Rural Housing Enabler' was born.

Against this background, rural housing associations began to mature. The change of the government in 1997 also brought another review of rural policy. In the years between the two reviews associations grew in numbers, in activity, in diversification, and in confidence.

New associations

In terms of numbers, there were not that many new associations. There were eleven new registrations in the period, of which only four followed the traditional route and created local associations in South Ayrshire, West Dunbartonshire, Perthshire and Stirlingshire. Five were in the Western Isles and were part of a new constellation model. The final two were to become the pioneers of associations created by the transfer of public sector stock – Pentland and Berwickshire. Rural Forum and Shelter had hoped that there would be at least one locally based association in each rural district and island area. This was not to be achieved in pre-reorganised local government, but the reduction of local authorities in 1997 saw that ambition realised!

The constellation model

Providing housing association development in the Western Isles demanded a different approach to anywhere else. With the principle of maximum local participation, a new model was tried. Five very small local associations were created – one in each of the main islands except North Uist. These were Barra & Vatersay, Berneray, Buidheann Tigheadas Na'Meadhanan (South Uist), Muirneag (Stornoway) Taighean Ceann A Tuath Na'Heradh (North Harris).

These associations employed no staff of their own, but bought in agency services from a larger unregistered association – Tighean Innse Gall. It was an attempt to provide economies of scale in the development and management of housing whilst local control and involvement were maintained through having a locally based association with a locally elected management committee. Some of the associations were very small with less than ten houses and were able to form their policies in the light of local circumstances.

Activity

Activity did increase. In the period between the two reviews, there was an increase in funding for social rented accommodation for rural associations. This was available for rehabilitation and new building. Over 6,200 houses were provided.in the period. But this has to be set against a reduction in Council building and the impact of Right to Buy. For every three houses built, ten were sold.

Diversity

Housing associations readily grasped the opportunities that the 1990 policy offered to diversify their offering to their communities. They rose to Sir James Mellon's 'one club golfer' challenge by demonstrating that they understood the need to provide a range of affordable housing through low cost home ownership initiatives. Care and Repair had become a major component for many associations. In 1988 this approach to helping older people improve their own homes was at pilot stage with projects run by Age Scotland and Shelter. By 1997 there were twenty-seven projects. For example, Lochalsh and Skye Housing Association had fourteen two-bedroom and three-bedroom bungalows available from February 1992 on a Shared Ownership basis. Potential buyers could purchase 25%, 50% or 75%, and prices started at £39,500. The Association then went on to introduce Rural Home Ownership Grants in November 1993. Equally important, Shelter, handed over administrative responsibility for the Skye & Lochalsh Care and Repair project to the Association in March 1993.

Confidence

Housing associations had an air of confidence about the future. Where they existed they were becoming embedded in their local communities as an accepted part of the rural infrastructure, alongside Local Economic Companies and Health Boards. They had local political support. There was more sophisticated analysis of local housing needs. How bright the future

Rural Workshop Homes – a Cautionary tale

It is clear that rural economic development requires houses for those who want to work in the countryside. Some housing associations have tried to provide workspaces. When East Lothian Housing Association inherited the East Saltoun and Dirleton developments from the Council they each had two workshops connected to the houses. We subsequently built two more at Stenton and one at Athelstaneford. The idea was sound – to encourage small businesses into rural villages by providing both a home and business premises. However, we received minimal HAG for the workshops, as a result of which the rents had to cover significant borrowing and so were very high. This meant that a small business had to earn a lot to cover the cost of premises. We have had some successes over the years and some really interesting businesses but the small 'cottage industry' type of business attracted to a rural village doesn't generally have the turnover to support the costs of the workshop. And if they do succeed we found that the tenants then wished to give up the tenancy in order to buy in the private market while still retaining the workshop. But originally the tenancy agreement bound the rented house and the workshop together. Long voids, high arrears or tenancies of short duration have generally been the result. After 1995 we built no more workshop homes and we are currently converting the workshops in East Saltoun into four housing units.

Peter Hayman, East Lothian Housing Association

was depended on a continuing supply of resources to meet those needs. The people resource – the voluntary committees and their staff – had the enthusiasm and the energy. The key resources they needed were land and money.

Land

Land remained a challenge. Indeed one association active in the Highlands told Rural Forum and Shelter in 1996 that *'the acquisition of land is probably the single most difficult problem facing a housing association developing in rural areas'*. Getting hold of land depended largely on the willingness of private landlords to sell. Planning permission needed to be obtained, and in many places, there was a presumption against development and in favour of the protection of the countryside, if not a lack of sympathy towards social housing. Then there was question of the cost of land – which was between 10 and 17% of total development costs in this period. There was the time it took to acquire land – three years was a common timescale. By that time it may be too late – for example jobs may have been lost because of a lack of housing. And once land had been identified and purchased, the cost of servicing small developments in more remote areas could prove very expensive. The easier option for associations was to build larger developments close to town on land that may have been acquired by the local authority or other public sector body that was willing to sell. But this meant further encouragement of movement away from villages and townships and the depopulation of the countryside. While rural associations had a role to play in market towns, was this to be at the expense of helping to sustain small rural communities?

Stock transfer

Pentland Housing Association is a good example of a locally based association that was originally set up specifically to take over public sector stock. Pentland was the first such rural association. It was not created to take over local authority or SSHA houses, but UK Atomic Energy Authority (UKAEA) houses in the Pennyland and Mount Vernon Estates in Thurso. UKAEA had decided to put the estates up for sale on the open market consisting of 350 tenanted houses and 474 rented garages, several common landscaped areas, and retained burdens for over 650 (approx.) privately owned houses. A Steering Group of tenants and residents was established and the newly formed Housing Association successfully bid for the estates and took ownership in January 1994.

The Association has built upon the success of acquisition of the UKAEA houses, develop housing in Wick and in the landward areas of Caithness, and now has a portfolio over 500 houses in the county.

In 1997 the Association was appointed as Agents by the Highland Council to establish and administer the new Care & Repair Scheme in Caithness. To complement this service up a Handyperson scheme was set up in 2005 to provide small repair services to the disabled and/or elderly residents in Caithness and Sutherland. Funded by the Highland Council this service continues to grow and in 2010 saw the addition of an adaptations store to provide services for Social Work.

The Association obtained charitable status in 2006 and formed a subsidiary company Pentland Community Enterprises to manage the extensive stock of garages. Further developments saw two other social enterprises offering a wide range of service and training opportunities for the local communities – Caithness Sports Facilities and Pentland Energy Advice.

Pentland works closely with other housing organisations in the Highlands. It holds representative Board Membership of the Highland Small Communities Trust and the Highland Housing and Community Care Trust. In 2005 the association formed the Highland Housing Alliance in partnership with the four other Highland based housing associations and The Highland Small Communities Housing Trust. As part of its commitment to the local area, the association is also a member of Caithness Voluntary Group and is represented on several other Highland and Caithness committees and voluntary organisations.

Money

Money for capital development, either in grants or loans, was never going to be enough. The period of the Housing Corporation and Scottish Homes had seen significant increase in funds. The great expansion of housing association activity that did not involve stock transfer took place during the eighteen years of Conservative Government. (The main stock transfer from Council housing to housing associations was to take place during the UK Labour Government and the early Scottish Parliament.) But although there had been an increase in available funds, the share of the Scottish Homes budget had not changed. And the main increase had been for low cost home ownership.

Would the challenges of land and money change with the new local government structure and the arrival of a new Labour government?

CHAPTER SIX

1997

A new Government

The fresh broom that swept into power in 1997 brought some new changes but much remained from before. The year before had seen the abolition of the District Council tier of local government. Housing was now only one of the services being supplied by Councils, rather being the main duty as it had been in the Districts. In some of the new Council areas like Highlands Council, Area Committees operated on similar geographical areas to the old Districts but with a wider interest. And rural housing associations, which were beginning to come to terms with the new local authority arrangements, now had to deal with a new Government whose strength lay in the urban central belt. What would the Labour Government's approach to rural communities be like?

Very soon remote rural Scotland had a champion in Brian Wilson who became the Scottish Office Minister for Education and Industry in 1997. He also had responsibility for the Highlands and Islands which allowed him to deliver on some of the issues that he had campaigned for over a long period. And the Government started to look seriously at land reform through the Land Reform Policy Group, set up in 1997, which eventually led to the Land Reform (Scotland) Act of 2003. Brian Wilson took the opportunity to establish the Community Land Unit and Fund within Highlands and Islands Enterprise, thus setting up the financial arrangements on which community buy-outs of crofting estates was based. He also set up Iomairt aig an Oir/Initiative at the Edge (IatE). This was designed to empower communities in some of Scotland's most remote and fragile areas, to identify their needs for area regeneration, consider what actions might be appropriate, and develop relevant projects in partnership with public sector agencies. One of the distinctive features of IatE was that there was no central source of funding and its success or otherwise depended overwhelmingly on the refocusing of the support given by public sector agencies working in partnership with community groups within the IatE areas. So land reform and a focus on supporting small and remote communities was a welcome development.

Housing policy in Scotland has always involved a large amount of consensus between Governments (the 1973–74 introduction of HAG is a clear example), but any new Government will add its own take. The new Government quickly published a discussion paper *Towards a Development Strategy for Rural Scotland*, emphasising partnership and bottom-up community led processes. Scottish Homes' overall policies were reexamined in that light, and a new strategy produced for 1997–2000. The Rural Policy was further reviewed. As part of the preparation for the rural review the Arkleton Centre had been commissioned to review the 1990 Rural Policy. The new Rural Policy Statement was issued in 1998. As before, it looked at a range of solutions and providers, although again, it was anticipated that housing associations would play the major part in its implementation.

'Scottish Homes continues to recognise the specific problems of rural areas and remains committed to meeting the challenges presented' was the opening phrase of the Statement. The rural challenge was located within the national *'themes of inclusion, leverage and quality, which would be achieved through partnership with public, private and voluntary organisations and empowerment of communities, tenants and staff'*. The Statement reinforced the diversity of rural Scotland; that housing provided a central focus to rural life; the need to tailor activities to the smaller scale of rural developments and to do so in partnership and in consultation with the community. One suggestion was to establish community development practitioners to support community involvement in housing solutions. Did this create the possibility of funding for Rural Housing Enablers? (Unfortunately this was never to happen.)

Although the review covered a wide range of issues and focused on communities, four other issues stand out. Land, wider role, quality and resource allocation.

Land – given the Government's land reform debate, the Statement picked up the particular rural dimension. It stressed the need for early dialogue regarding what was being termed 'sustainable community ownership' and raised the issues of what public/private resources were available from partners to meet community aspirations and to support community involvement and empowerment. It made some useful proposals about public land being sold to housing associations at lower than market value; the use of its CPO powers to compulsorily acquire land where these was an agreement with key partners at a local level; and whether Scottish Homes should develop a landbank.

Wider Role – in many ways this was a development of what associations were already undertaking. The phrase 'Wider Role' was used to describe supplementary activity by associations aimed at improving the physical, social or economic environment. Included were local employment, energy efficiency, and information and advice programmes.

Quality – featured the traditional issues about the existing stock. There was a strong push for Care and Repair, and for measures involving the private rented sector such as lead tenancies, and Rural Empty Homes Grants. It also featured the question of standards for new house building, building on research that had been carried out including energy efficiency, barrier free access, materials, construction techniques and design. John Richards, who had been chair of the Scottish Committee of the Housing Corporation and the Deputy Chairman of Scottish Homes had, along with his wife Margaret, produced in 1994 an excellent report and guide on *Timber Frame Houses in the Scottish Countryside* as part of the research.

Resources – the Arkleton evaluation had recommended an increase in the rural share of resources and the need for a clearly articulated rationale for resource distribution. The response involved the proposal for a three-year strategy document creating Regional Plans which would have a specific rural focus. The framework would explain the regional distribution between urban and rural. It suggested that it would be useful to have a common definition within which 'rural' investment could be accurately measured and assessed. The resource allocation system being developed would take into account social exclusion and performance criteria to encourage innovation and value for money. There was a recognition that social exclusion in rural areas was more difficult to assess, being more individual than group and that the nature of rural housing development may require modifications to the criteria. Although nothing was said about increasing resources for rural areas, the indication was that resources would be sustained at a level consistent with previous years.

While not quite 'business as usual', the prospects looked good. But the biggest external change was still to come. In September 1997, three quarters of the Scottish electorate voted for devolution of powers from Westminster to a reconvened Scottish Parliament. Although separate housing legislation had existed for years for Scotland, and its implementation managed by civil servants in Edinburgh, many in the housing association sector thought that devolution might be an opportunity for a both a higher political profile and for even more local solutions. With the creation of Scottish Homes, there had been no formal link with Government housing bodies in England and Wales. The prospect was that at least it should be easier to access the new decision making processes, which should also be less cumbersome and hopefully more open to ideas and to influence.

CHAPTER SEVEN

1999

Parliament

1 July 1999. The Scottish Parliament reconvened after 292 years. The Scottish Executive (as the Government in Scotland was to be known in the early days of devolution) was a coalition between Labour and Liberal Democrats, and early in its life published a Green Paper *Investing in Modernisation – an Agenda for Scotland's Housing*, setting out a basis for discussion on future housing policy. Significantly, this was the first Green Paper on housing for over twenty years, and signaled the return of housing to the political agenda. It was followed up by a series of task forces and consultation events that fulfilled the early promise of a different approach to the development of policy. This led, after consultation, to a White Paper *Better Homes for Scotland's Communities*, and then to the Housing (Scotland) Act 2001. It was a further sign of devolution. But not all 'housing' resources were devolved; the main omission being Housing Benefit which was retained by Westminster.

The framework within which housing associations had to operate was to become quite different under devolution from that in the 1990s. One of the changes was the demise of Scottish Homes and the creation of Communities Scotland as an Executive Agency of the Scottish Executive in 2001. This reflected the position of housing within the new Government. Housing became effectively a subset of a ministerial portfolio that included social inclusion, area regeneration, and planning. Communities Scotland had responsibility for regulation of RSLs and local authorities in the provision of social housing, and for supporting the social economy to deliver key services and create job opportunities. In some ways this was a logical development of the approach that had started by the Labour Government in 1997 and featured in the 1998 Rural Policy Statement, including the Wider Action programme.

With those changes, any separate rural housing policy at Government level disappeared, although the Government's rural commitment was overseen by Environment and Rural affairs Department (SEERAD) which became responsible for rural development, but not economic development and therefore not responsible for agencies like HIE. The lack of coordination of housing, economic and rural development was potentially a missed opportunity.

The big issue that housing policy centered on after devolution was related to the under-investment in council housing – particularly in the urban central belt. The quality was poor, as was often the relationship between tenants and landlord. This was to be tackled primarily by transfers of public sector stock to 'community ownership' landlords, of which the housing association model was seen as key. Transfer would allow additional investment (mainly through private funding) and it offered tenants the opportunity of having a management role. The main vehicle for achieving this was to be through New Housing Partnerships. Again this was a development of work which Scottish Homes had pioneered.

Stock transfer was to become a major feature of the housing association sector and not just in urban areas. Rural areas saw some of the earliest transfers and some of the major transfers. The community ownership programme involved tenants voting to transfer their homes out of the public sector to a housing association. A number of existing associations acquired houses inherited by Scottish Homes from SSHA. New associations were created to take on the entire housing stock of the Council, following the example of Pentland and Berwickshire. A number of councils considered transferring their whole stock, and five transfers were carried out – four in rural areas. The second largest stock transfer in Scotland (after Glasgow Housing Association) was to Dumfries and Galloway Housing Partnership and involved 11,900 houses. Three other rural local authorities transferred their entire stock to newly created housing associations – Argyll, Comhairle an Eilean Siar and Scottish Borders, giving four rural authorities with no housing stock, and dependent on associations to provide all the social rented housing in their area.

The 2001 Act had other impacts including the development of Common Housing Registers and a single Scottish Secure Tenancy. Local authorities were required to produce Local Housing Strategies. There was to be a strategy for the prevention and alleviation of homelessness, with associations having a duty to assist and can only refuse to provide accommodation where there is 'good reason'. Right to Buy was extended to tenants who did not have the right, but excluded housing associations with charitable status and was not to come into force for ten years. Significantly (particularly in rural areas) local authorities could apply for exemption from RTB for five years by securing 'Pressured Area Status' in certain areas.

Further legislation was to follow that would affect rural associations, including reforms to the Scottish Feudal tenure system, to the management of tenements, and to land ownership. Legislation on housing became a regular feature of the Parliament. For example, in 2003 the Parliament took the radical step of setting the objective that everyone assessed as unintentionally homeless would be entitled to permanent accommodation by 2012.

The Title Conditions (Scotland) Act 2003 enabled the introduction in 2004 of Rural Housing Burdens (RHB). This development resulted from an initiative from Di Alexander and his Highland colleagues. RHBs were to become another addition to the range of measures that help to make land available, and therefore make it easier to provide affordable housing - in this case for home ownership. Under the mechanism, land is acquired at a discounted rate, and the discount is passed on for the benefit of the local community. To operate the system, the housing association or the Community Land Trust has to first be designated as a 'rural housing body' by the Government. Then the designated body acquires a piece of land at a discounted rate from a landowner and builds houses on the land. When the houses are sold, a RHB is inserted into the Title Deeds, giving the designated body the right to re-purchase the property whenever it is made available for sale. In this way the discount is locked in forever, and the houses remain within the local affordable market rather than being 'lost' to the open market.

The inclusion of Community Land Trusts (CLTs) in the RHB mechanism reflected the important role that the Development Trust movement was to play in rural development – particularly in the Highlands and Islands where 'Community Right to Buy' by CLTs of private estates has become such an important part of the regeneration of rural Scotland. This was one of the main outcomes from the land reform review that had led to the Land Reform Act 2003.

In the Highlands, another initiative had been developed to help secure land for housing association development. In 1998, Di Alexander, having set up Lochaber Housing Association was involved with establishing the Highlands Small Communities Housing Trust (HSCHT) with the strong support of Jill Stewart, Highland Council's Head of Strategy. It created a Council wide land banking facility. A start up grant from the Scottish Executive enabled a revolving fund; sites were acquired and then sold to individuals with RHOG support or to housing associations. It has now grown to be a major player in the Highlands, both working with housing associations and complementing them by providing services house plots and providing housing for key workers.

A further development of the Trust was the Highland Housing Alliance (HHA), a development company working in partnership with the Highland Council, housing associations, Scottish Government, private landowners and developers to help build more homes of all tenures for people in the Highlands. It is owned by five housing associations, the HSCHT and the Council. It too has grown to become a major player In the Highland Council Area, as a developer, and as a manager of private rented housing.

In 2006, the 'Tolerable Standard' which had been the 'condemnation standard' for over forty years had the additional criteria of thermal insulation and electrical installations added. This reflected a recognition that had been growing over the years of the need to tackle the level of fuel poverty in Scotland and the concerns about the impact of climate change. The primary concern was fuel poverty. The cost of fuel in rural Scotland is higher than elsewhere and, coupled with poor insulation, unregulated bottled gas and thus the dependence on electricity gives rural communities higher levels of fuel poverty. Associations recognised this and developed ways of improving the situation through information and advice to tenants and, but also leading with renewable energy. Some, like Lochalsh and Skye Housing Association have developed Energy advice projects for the community part financed by the Climate Challenge Fund and the European Community Highland LEADER programme.

Sustainable housing design incorporating energy efficiency, low carbon building processes and value for money developed as a key issue during the first decade of the twenty-first century. Since the Richards' report on Timber Housing in the Countryside, many developments in rural Scotland have demonstrated sympathetic, high quality modern design. Award winning

A Leader in Energy Efficiency

Lochalsh and Skye Housing Association won a Highly Commended award at the 2007 National Energy Efficiency Awards in London in recognition of its work towards improving energy efficiency and reducing carbon emissions and fuel poverty.

The Association installed heat pumps at its new properties at Home Farm, and was constructing a district heating scheme which would serve 128 homes and be fuelled by locally-sourced timber. Low-energy light bulbs and Power Down devices were also being given – free of charge – to Association tenants.

At the EAS Energy Savers Award 2008 run by fuel poverty charity Energy Action Scotland and supported by eaga, the Association won Scotland's top award for its energy efficiency commitment in general. Presenting the

award, Jackie Baillie, MSP, Dumbarton, described the Association's energy efficiency work as 'a shining light to other housing providers'.

Lochalsh and Skye HA energy award.
Photo from Lochalsh and Skye Association

architectural practices have flourished, encouraged by housing associations. And associations have encouraged modern building practices as well.

In 2010, Inverness hosted the first (and so far the only) housing expo in Scotland. *'Scotland's Housing Expo in 2010 was the first of its kind in the UK. It demonstrates a creative response to the desire for innovation and encouraged the exploration of new housing standards for sustainable design, innovative construction, energy efficiency and the use of low Carbon and renewable systems and technologies'.* It represented a brave new world of better design, optimism in the future of housing quality and a recognition that not everything should happen in the central belt. Prompted by the Scottish Government's desire to bring the Finnish model of a Housing Expo to Scotland, Highland Council initiated the project with the active support of the Scottish Government, Sust. – the Government's Sustainability in Architecture Programme, Forestry Commission Scotland, Royal Incorporation of Architects in Scotland (RIAS), Highlands and

The challenge of building houses on an island without a roll on-roll off ferry.
The kit for two houses is delivered at North Ronaldsay, the most northerly island
in Orkney. With a population of just sixty the community badly needed families with
primary school age children (the local primary school was in danger of closing)
and adults able to take up some of the vacant jobs in the island. The build was
exceptionally expensive but the impact on and benefits to the community were
immeasurable. Orkney Housing Association created a new demand
(by promoting an island life style) rather than meet an existing one.
Photo Orkney HA

Islands Enterprise, Highland Birchwoods, Homes for Scotland and Inverness Architectural Association. Highland Housing Alliance (HHA) were responsible for the implementation with Cadell2 (now known as AREA) as their appointed masterplanners.

However, by 2010, the dark cloud of recession hung over the Expo and other developments. And more political change heralded even more radical challenges for housing associations.

CHAPTER EIGHT

2010

Firm Foundations?

The Holyrood Elections in 2007 saw a minority SNP Scottish Government (name changed immediately from Scottish Executive) with a majority SNP Scottish Government being elected in 2011. Very soon after taking office for the first time the Government issued a discussion paper *Firm Foundations – the Future of Housing in Scotland,* which ultimately led to the Housing (Scotland) Act 2010. Much of the content had been inherited from the previous administration; yet more continuity in housing policy. While the discussion was under way, Communities Scotland was abolished as an agency in 2008 and its responsibilities transferred to Scottish Government Housing and Regeneration Directorate; in turn it became part of the Communities Directorate. An interim Scottish Housing Regulator was formed, to be formally established when the Act became law (and accountable to the parliament and not ministers), along with the Scottish Social Housing Charter, while housing associations and cooperatives were defined as Registered Social Landlords (RSLs).

The Government's proposals included increasing national supply from 25,000 new houses per year to 35,000 while improving its quality by, amongst other measures:

- incentivising local authorities to build council housing once again;
- ending the right to buy for new social housing;
- awarding subsidies to associations on a strategic and competitive basis;
- establishing a Scottish Housing Quality Standard;
- promoting new stand-alone sustainable communities;
- broaden the financial products to help home ownership;
- helping the private rented sector play a full role in 'meeting housing need in urban and <u>rural</u> areas through the provision of good quality accommodation for private rent'.

An ambitious agenda, much of which was delivered in the 2010 Act. However, the well intentioned plan was thrown into turmoil as the economy went into recession, and Government capital investment cut by 29% over a three year period. Nevertheless, the Government continued to work towards a target of 30,000 per year, and set up the Housing Supply Task Force to look at how the target could be met, including a number of reforms to the planning system, alternative funding methods, and better use of publicly owned land. Housing in rural Scotland was identified as an early priority, with lessons to be learnt from work undertaken, not least by the Prince's Foundation, which had published a report that identified many examples where the private sector had played an important role in the delivery of affordable rural housing. There was no direct mention of housing associations and the innovative roles they were playing. Housing Association Grant (HAG) benchmark levels were reduced, while other incentives, including a 'Rural homes for Rent' designed for the private sector was introduced. It looked as if the new Government was more interested in developing the private sector than building upon an existing success story. It also appeared that the paper was written with more of an urban audience in mind.

While rural housing was mentioned only in passing in *Firm Foundations*, it became an early issue for review by the Parliament's Rural Affairs and Environment Committee. This was a wide ranging review which started with the recognition that there was a *'serious affordable housing problem'*, and that to some extent rural Scotland was a *'victim of its own success'*, with increased population and more economic activity. The main problem was simply put by the Committee in its report – *'there are not enough houses in many areas'*.

The committee began by criticising the planning system for having an over-cautious culture that effectively entrenched a presumption against development. It called for a cultural change; the Government's response was to attempt to change the culture by revising planning guidance that supported appropriate housing development in rural areas, including outside recognised settlements. Since then local authorities have been required to set out affordable housing policies in Planning Advice Note 2/2010.

Land availability, as could be expected, formed a major part of the Committee's consideration. A variety of issues were considered, including the question of zoning more land for housing, and for even creating an 'Affordable Housing' use class (the latter had been argued for by a number of bodies, but was rejected by the Committee). Land banking was supported, with the model of the Highland Housing Alliance (HHA) being particularly commended. A more robust approach was required to the acquisition of land; the committee regarded the use of Compulsory Purchase Powers as 'under-used', and encouraged its use under certain circumstances, including land zoned for housing which had minimal agricultural use, the development of which would be for community benefit.

In looking at the issue of Government funding for affordable housing, the Committee reviewed its then new 'Affordable Housing Investment Programme', of which HAG was the largest element. The members commented that the spending plans *'do not take sufficiently into account the need of rural Scotland, and that the increased costs of building houses for rural areas have been underestimated'.* This was supported by evidence from HHA and Scottish Borders Council, which reported *'. . . it seems as if funding is prioritised towards communities that offers economies of scale, [and] large settlements and can support flagship regeneration projects.'* While recognising that demand for efficiencies in the HAG system were understandable, the Committee reminded the Government that economies of scale were easier to achieve in an urban context and *'there is a risk that an over-dogmatic pursuit of the approach in rural areas could lead to a decline in the influence of local housing associations with a corresponding risk that local communities' views will not be properly heard . . . greater use of bulk procurement could squeeze out small-scale local contractors.'* The Committee well understood the rural challenges.

More support for a distinctive rural approach to housing came from an international and highly respected source. The OECD Rural Policy Reviews included Scotland in 2008. It concluded that rural areas showed better socioeconomic and wellbeing indicators than urban areas, but when it came to housing it highlighted the issue of land, both its availability and what it termed 'a rigid regulation of land use'. It commented

'In Scotland, landowners, especially large ones, have found an important source of rent from protectionist policies and later in the CAP, and this support in turn capitalized in higher values for their land. For this and other reasons, landowners have often little interest in selling or diversifying their activities. The

National Planning Framework does stress that economic diversification is vital to the future of rural Scotland and policies have used indirect instruments to facilitate rural housing (like subsidizing social housing for low income families or other priority groups or the cost of ferries that haul building materials). This bottleneck would be better addressed directly instead of indirectly through other instruments'.

The Affordable Housing Investment Programme (AHIP) brought together all the Government's funding programmes for both rent and low cost home ownership. Local authorities Local Housing Strategies have an annual Strategic Housing Investment Plan (SHIP) which sets out how they plan to prioritise for delivery of objectives sets out in the Strategy. Although HAG was the largest element in AHIP, the amount per house was reducing, with a greater call on private finance and a resultant impact on rents. By the beginning of 2010, HAG had reduced to £65,000. However the Government had listened to the Rural Affairs and Environment Committee, amongst others, and had increased the rural HAG to £70,000. But HAG was to reduce further, with the result, in many cases, of reduced development programmes, and for some associations no further development programme.

'Fresh Thinking'

No sooner had the 2010 Act been introduced, the Government introduced the next policy paper *'Homes fit for the 21st Century'*. This followed a discussion paper *'Housing: Fresh Thinking, New Ideas'* and heralded an even more radical approach to housing procurement. It reflected the ambition to improve the quality of both older and new housing and the financial reality that the Government would not have sufficient resources itself to deliver the scale of programme needed. Critically two phrases sum up the position about new building – *'we cannot rely on the traditional methods used to finance new homes'* and *'we will implement a radically different and innovative approach'*.

The proposals as they were worked out involved an entirely different approach to producing houses. This envisaged large scale procurement with complex financial packaging. Not all lending institutions which had supported the sector survived the recession. The Dunfermline Building

Society was one which had supported associations over the years, and which had to be taken over by Nationwide. Those that did survive placed heavier demands on associations, and it became more expensive to borrow.

The impact of all the legislative and financial changes since devolution has had a dramatic impact on the sector. The speed of change was almost breathtaking. While the number of houses in housing association/RSL ownership grew rapidly through stock transfer, the pressure for greater efficiency in the sector led to structural changes. The days of high levels of Housing Association Grant had come to an end, indeed the name has disappeared. Private finance has become a way of life, requiring more sophistication in forward planning and financial management. Since the financial crisis, lenders have made greater demands upon borrowers.

The demand for efficiency led to reduced costs, both in capital and in revenue. A number of smaller associations were not viable as independent organisations, and mergers began. Names like Dunan Housing Cooperative (in Dunoon) disappeared, having been merged with Isle of Bute (and with other mergers that became Fyne Homes); East Perthshire merged with Perthshire (and again more mergers led to Caledonia); Isle of Cumbrae with Cunninghame; Carrick with Ayrshire. More were to come, including the disappearance of the constellation model and the small associations in the Western Isles. With the creation in 2006 of the Hebridean Housing Partnership by the transference of the Comhairle an Eilean Siar's housing stock, the local very small associations were absorbed into the larger body.

Those RSLs that remained looked at different ways of procuring housing, and of developing different ways of delivering housing services to local communities. Sharing services between RSLs had been a feature for years, but now some began to look at either sharing or buying in development services. Many rural associations that had built up their own development teams had to close them down and start to buy services from larger RSLs. Others stopped developing. As for other kinds of services, some RSLs divested themselves of Care and Repair projects, but others not only developed them, but extended into Handyman Projects with finance from Local authorities and the local NHS.

In the midst of the changes, partnership had become even more essential for delivering housing. For RSLs this did not only mean working with public sector bodies. Other players in rural housing worked closely with the sector, indeed there was much inter-relationship within what was known by 2003 as social enterprise sector, and new social enterprises were set up by associations themselves.

Voluntary organisations that had had a long term relationship with the housing association sector continued to play their part. Shelter provided housing advice and led on the Empty Homes Initiative. SHARC – Shelter Housing Action with Rural Communities – continued to raise issues in Dumfries and Galloway culminating in the creation of Dumfries & Galloway Small Communities Housing Trust. Rural Forum, which had played such an important role in helping raise the profile of rural housing and instigating initiatives including housing associations had to be wound up in 1999. But its housing project was rescued by Scottish Churches Housing Action and then became the independent Rural Housing Scotland (RHS). Before its crash, Rural Forum had pioneered working with communities to develop their own affordable housing for local people and in doing so brought a number of agencies and opportunities together. One of the earliest projects was at Laggan, where the local community through their Community Trading Company ran the local shop, and also bought and renovated five empty formerly Forest Commission houses, with help from Albyn Housing Society, Highland Council, RHS and with the first ever loan in Scotland from Triodos Bank (yet another partnership that was to grow in importance). When the Gigha community bought the island in 2002 using the 'community buy out' process and with the support of the Scottish Land Fund and HIE, they inherited a number of houses in need of improvement and repair. Grants were available for improvement and repair, but no grants for them to build new houses which were needed to house a growing population. RHS arranged for the Gigha Trust to make land available at low cost so that Fyne Homes could build eighteen new homes. Rural development demands partnership in many ways!

While committees continued to focus on providing housing and housing related services to local and vulnerable communities, they have had to learn so many new ways of working. The financial regime required new business skills. The Regulator required a very high level of accountability to tenants.

As the present moves into the future, RSL innovation continues. The latest initiative involves Albyn Housing Society and a new model delivery mechanism. The National Housing Trust was set up with support from

Rural Housing Scotland – launching from collapse

One Saturday morning in May 1999, as I idly browsed *The Scotsman* over a cup of coffee, I got a shock. I read that the Board of Rural Forum, the umbrella body for a myriad of activities and interests in rural Scotland, had decided to wind the organisation up. The incoming Chief Executive had looked at the books and realised his predecessor had left behind an unviable set-up. The organisation was trading beyond its means, so dissolution became inevitable.

I was involved. I was a member of the advisory group supporting the housing project, staffed by Derek Logie – a group led by Raymond Young, who had recently joined the Board of Rural Forum "Sorry to hear you're going to be redundant," I said to Derek on the phone. "Any help I can offer?" (As one does, little thinking the answer might be yes . . .). "Well, actually," said Derek. "I think we can save the housing project – if we can find an organisation to take us on."

It transpired that the Scottish Office – as it then was, as this was a matter of weeks before the Parliament opened – had allocated a year's money for the project, but had only paid across the first quarter's instalment. The rest was safe from the administrator's hands.

Scottish Churches Housing Action was then – as it still is – a small organisation, seeking to travel light. Could we take on this project? Would it cost us? Would it divert us from our main task? Would we get dragged into a financial mess, as Rural Forum had?

Any Chairman worth his salt would ask these questions and more when faced with an enthusiastic member of staff wanting to push something through. And George McArthur, our Chairman at the time, was a man of the old school. He was cautious and saw pitfalls, reluctant when I saw only opportunities. The factor that allowed him to give the proposal the green light was one name: Raymond Young. George had been in charge of Kirk Care Housing Association, and had served as Chairman of Scottish Federation of Housing Associations when Raymond had held various senior positions in Scottish Homes. There was trust between them. I highlight this neither to boost Raymond's ego (which hardly needs it . . .), nor to exalt the merits of the old boys' club: rather to illustrate how trust can short-cut processes. A small country like Scotland builds up social capital through acquaintances and friendships. Of course that needs to be moderated to ensure it doesn't descend into sloppiness and nepotism, but when urgent action is needed it certainly can help.

Highland Small Communities Housing Trust development at Kincraig.
Photo: Highland Small Communities Housing Trust

Di Alexander.
Photo: Scottish Federation of Housing Associatons

Highland Small Communities Housing Trust development at Fodderty, by Dingwall.
Photo: Highland Small Communities Housing Trust

Lochaber Housing Association's development at Arisaig.
Photo: Lochaber Housing Association

The longest serving housing association committee member? In 1961, Bobby Reid joined the William Woodhouse Strain Housing Association Committee which subsequently merged with Isle of Bute Housing Association in 2002 to become Fyne Homes Ltd. He retired in 2014 after 53 years. Colin Renfrew, Fyne Homes Chief Executive, gives him a retirement present.

Photo: Fyne Homes

Typical Rothesay renovations – before and after.

Photo: Fyne Homes

Another pioneer. D A Morrison, whose work with Lochalsh
and Skye Housing Association was recognised by the award
of an MBE and the association's offices named after him.

Photo: Lochalsh and Skye Housing Association

Charles Kennedy MP performs the opening ceremony of the
six houses at Cnoc a'Chonaisg, Ardvaser in September 1986.

Photo: Lochalsh and Skye Housing Association

I subsequently heard that Liz Nicholson at Shelter Scotland was a bit miffed that we at SCHA had moved first: we said yes while she was awaiting permission from head office in London. So Derek worked in our (very urban) office in Albany Street in Edinburgh, with scarcely a break in his salary, for the next eighteen months. The Tudor Trust came in with some crucial funds to supplement the Scottish Executive (as it by then was) money. We looked at various scenarios, and decided that a free-standing charity was the best way forward.

Raymond and I were signatories on the memorandum of the new organisation, along with Peter Pearson of Rural Stirling Housing Association. The first assembly of the new body took place in Perth on Saturday 3 February 2001.

03.02.01 – not a bad date for a launch.

the Scottish Futures Trust (SFT) to leverage in private sector funding and to enable local authorities to work with private developers to provide homes at intermediate rent levels. Once complete, a local partnership company comprising the developer, the local authority and SFT buys the homes and lets them at affordable, mid-market rent for a period of five to ten years after which the houses are sold. Highland Housing Alliance was one of the first to act as developer in the programme, and now Albyn is testing an RSL variant, within which the Scottish Government guarantees the debt element for five years, and then RSL has to decide to keep the homes (without the guarantee), sell, or do a mixture of both. It is an indication of the complexity and innovation that is now required to meet the challenge of providing homes in the twenty-first century. It is a far cry from the days when William Woodhouse Strain built eight houses using land and money that was bequeathed. But will it solve the problem?

Before looking to the future, it is time to listen to other voices, to some of the voluntary committee members and staff.

PART TWO

The voices

Author's Introduction to Part Two

When this book was first considered, the plan was to weave into the text some shorter pieces from individuals. This would demonstrate the importance of personal commitment, energy and shared vision used to sustain the effort of creating and maintaining the kind of associations which make significant contributions to potentially fragile local communities. Some of these have been included in Part One. Other people offered to write more about their association and its beginnings. Instead of weaving these stories into the overview, the view has been taken that these are best presented as stand-alone stories in their own right. Some are short; others are long. There has been minimal editing – in some case to make cross reference to part of the story in the overview.

When telling stories about organisations, there are often three questions that people have to ask. Why did it start, who initiated it, and what helped it get going? In the first group of these stories, the origins are explained – some in more in more detail than others. In all cases, the association has matured over the years, but not without some difficulties on its journey, and some of the more difficult moments are recounted as well. Then there is a story of the early days of Care and Repair. And finally, these are followed by two longer pieces – one a more detailed story of one association, and the other of housing association developments in a whole region.

More important is how these stories humanise an otherwise bureaucratic and political history. They tell of people living in poor housing conditions or none, and of others who have been moved by these conditions to devote their energies to improving the housing opportunities for individuals and communities.

Out of tiny acorns . . .

Angus Housing Association

*Angus Housing Association is one of the oldest rural based associations in Scotland, created long before the Housing Corporation or Scottish Homes. Its story reflects the changing environment which associations have faced over the years and how they have adapted to survive. And it is a tale of small rural beginnings which led to urban involvement. Association Secretary **Elizabeth Whitson**, who has been a Committee Member since 1977 and a past Chairman tells the story.*

Elizabeth Whitson.
Photo by Angus Whitson

In the 1960s the north east fishing village of Auchmithie, four miles north of Arbroath, was a decaying village with no mains water or sewerage system, a few old fishermen's cottages, and a small, inter-related close knit community. What had been a thriving fishing community in the middle of the nineteenth century began to dwindle as the attraction of a good harbour, no arduous toiling up and down the cliff path to the harbour in Auchmithie, and better housing caused the migration of many of the residents to Arbroath.

According to the 1961 Census, Auchmithie had a population of 115, but by 1969 was only served by three WC's connected to septic tanks, along with a number of chemical toilets in inhabited premises. Most of the village and the surrounding land was owned by the local farmer Mrs. Nell Grant, and her son Allan, and the houses were factored for them by Property Factors in Dundee owned by a Mr. Malcolm Curry.

At a Mess Dinner during a Territorial Army camp in the late sixties, three men, one of them the housing factor keen to do something about the state of the village, a lawyer, and an accountant had a conversation about Auchmithie and the possibility of funding becoming available to form a new concept called a Housing Association. Malcolm Curry was the driving force behind the idea – he would manage the houses. The lawyer, George Mathieson, would deal with the administration of the Association and the accountant Neil Sharp, would be the Auditor

Allan Grant was a County Councillor at the time, and Angus County Council agreed to put a main sewer and water into Auchmithie, but not while the village was so rundown. With the Council's help the Housing Association was established with a view to improving the existing houses and building new cottages in the gap sites. In 1970 the Auchmithie Housing Association was born with Mrs. Nell Grant as Chairman.

With the assistance of the then Head of Planning at Dundee College of Art, a plan was submitted to Angus County Council for a new build and rehabilitation scheme. It was supported by the Council, but due to design and planning difficulties for the new houses, it was almost three years before it got underway. George Mathieson tells the story that when the bulldozers came in to start clearing the site for the new build houses, residents lay down in front of them in an effort to stop the building. When the scheme was completed it gave the Association forty-nine houses – six gap site new builds, three rehabilitated and forty new build houses on the edge of the village.

The name soon changed to Angus Housing Association; having started in Auchmithie, further development was envisaged outside the village, and initially in Arbroath.

By 1979 the keys of the 100th house were handed over in Fergus Square, Arbroath after the Association had carried out rehabilitation schemes in Arbroath and Montrose and had a further eight rehabilitation schemes in the planning stages.

I joined the Committee in 1977 after the Association had started to develop in Montrose. The Committee was quite small then. Mrs. Nell Grant was still Chairman and Alan Grant a Committee member. There was always a representative from Council who was Mrs. Ella Cargill. Mr. George Payne, a retired banker who became the second Chairman. Representing the historical links with Auchmithie, Mr. Tom Girth whose mother had funded the building of the village hall – The Anne Girth Memorial Hall. Tom had retired from Falkland Islands Trading Company and returned to live in Arbroath. There was also a tenant member from Auchmithie village, and I was asked to join as I was based in Montrose. The meetings were held on Wednesday mornings in the Boardroom of our lawyer's office in Arbroath. I was self-employed, and other members were retired or available during the day. The architects, surveyors and factor also joined us until our numbers increased and we outgrew the round table!

As well as opening our 100th house in 1979, the restoration of Newgate House, the oldest house in Arbroath, was approved. It's interesting to note that twenty years before, Arbroath Town Council had applied to the Historic Buildings Council for Scotland for a grant for the preservation of Newgate House which had been refused. In 1977 Angus District Council asked the Housing Association if they would be interested in carrying out a scheme for the property. The Association obtained agreement with the proprietors of the ground and first floors to sell. Renovations were subject to retaining the original stonework, and there were rigorous rules about internal alterations and we were concerned that the house should be restored as near as possible to its original state. Angus District Council gave a grant of £15,000, and HBC gave a similar amount. The overall cost of the scheme, which provides four two apartment flats on the first and second floor cost £67,160.00 – what would that buy now!

The Housing Corporation was by then our principal funder, as well as private finance, and the ratio of HAG to private finance was very favourable with grant subsidies at a realistic level. But we did bite our nails every year waiting to find out what our funding allocation was going to be. Finding land and properties wasn't too difficult in hindsight, and most sites were brought to our attention by the Council. In the early days it was Angus County Council who suggested the sites we should develop and who provided the grant funding.

Newgate House Arbroath.
Photo from Angus HA

In the minutes of September 1988 it was recorded that Angus District Council had asked the Association to look at the site of the old Arbroath Swimming Pool and a feasibility study should be undertaken. The building would be demolished, keeping the Victorian facade with new housing built behind it . . . After seven years of planning and negotiation, demolition began in June 1993, and the £1 million redevelopment programme began.

Also in 1988 the ongoing schemes recorded were the conversion of Hospital field Farm Steading, a Terrace house in Hill Place in Arbroath. A conversion at Hamilton Green in Arbroath and a new build scheme in the village of Ferrymen just outside Montrose. The District Council had a site in the village of Letham and were in the process of identifying a housing need.

Hospital field Farm Steading on the edge of Arbroath was converted into flats and bed sits, and we created an interesting round house from the old horse mill. The land adjoining the rehab was then developed into housing in our first ever joint venture with Gowrie Housing Association. Together we completed a £2.3 million development of fifty-two houses – thirty for rent and twenty-two for sale under the low cost home ownership scheme officially opened in 1994.

In 1990 we merged with East of Scotland Housing Association. This was a small Association with housing in Barnhill on the outskirts of Dundee, which had become too small to be viable. We then became Angus and East of Scotland Housing Association and took on ownership and management of the rented housing remaining after the Right to buy had removed some of their stock. The first joint Committee meeting was held on 14 March 1990 and committee members from East of Scotland joined us.

Arbroath always had, and still does have a housing need. The purchase of five blocks of redundant MOD flats in the Cliff burn area of Arbroath added quickly to our housing stock. These were renovated. And a large play area created. Over the years these proved to be expensive to maintain, asbestos was found in the construction and had to be removed and they have now been demolished and new housing developed on the site.

The old Court House in Arbroath was obsolete and we converted that into flats. There were particular difficulties to overcome when dividing the building horizontally due to the height of the court room.

A disused Billiard Hall was converted into flats, retaining the shops underneath, and a number of properties in the High Street were acquired and turned into flats.

In 1992 the Association opened the Jubilee Park development in the village of Letham. This was a new build development offering the first shared ownership houses in rural Angus incorporating thirteen rented and four shared ownership homes.

By this time, the number of Committee members had increased to give a wider range of professional members and a number of our tenants. We had to move our meetings out of Thornton's Board Room into Arbroath Library, and receive reports from consultants who no longer attended the Committee meetings. Our first meeting in the Library was held in September 1992.

In 1993 a survey by Scottish Homes showed that people were being forced away from their rural localities by lack of suitable housing. After close consultation with the local community and Angus District Council; the Association produced a plan for eight houses in Deadhead in the Angus Glens.

At Condor Crescent on the outskirts of Montrose, Angus District Council owned properties originally built to provide housing for RAF personnel. Angus and East of Scotland Housing Association joined forces with Hillcrest Housing Association for a £3 million development of the land adjoining Condor Crescent with the emphasis on environmental improvements and extensive landscaping. The Council reduced the number of homes originally proposed to accommodate a larger playground, and they upgraded the houses they owned to bring the standard in line with the new build homes

By the early nineties we had a pool of architects, surveyors and contractors who were called on depending on what type of development we were planning, but funding was becoming more difficult, and just not coming our way. We were now regulated by Scottish Homes and by this time, most Housing Associations had their own employed staff and were run by housing professionals. Our administration, funding applications and development, and housing management was still carried out by the original consultants – the lawyers and the housing factors.

Scottish Homes, who owned and managed the SSHA housing in Scotland, decided they no longer wanted to be landlords, and their housing stock was to be transferred to Housing Associations and Cooperatives.

Little housing associations like ours did not fit into that pattern, and our development funding was withdrawn. Unless we radically changed our structure we would either be subsumed into a bigger organisation, or remain as a purely managing Association.

This was a difficult time. Some of the Committee members were totally against change and against employing our own staff of housing professionals to be in a position to join the bid for the Stock Transfer, which, if we were successful, could overnight almost double our housing stock. We were approached by both Hillcrest and Gowrie Housing Associations with the view to 'merging' and declined their offers!

I was Chairman at this time – only the third Chairman in the History of the Association – and we needed help. This came from John Kernighan of Perthshire Housing Association – an experienced housing professional. Perthshire Housing Association were appointed as Consultants to help us develop our future strategy. The decision was taken finally to employ staff, and to draw up a bid for the Scottish Homes Stock Transfer; to revert to being Angus Housing Association, to purchase our own offices and sever the ties with our consultants. Malcolm Currie and Neil Sharp had both retired in 1993 after twenty-three years of service to the Association. George Mathieson and his firm Thornton's were still our Managing Agents, and it was with sadness that we bade farewell to them after twenty-five years.

Scottish Homes then reinstated our development status and we began to recruit our first members of staff, still employing the help of John Kernighan and Alison Crook. The first appointment was the Director. This was, and still is Bruce Forbes – previously Director of Ormiston Peoples Cooperative in Whitfield, Dundee. 93 High Street Arbroath, a three story Victorian building which had been a solicitor's office was purchased in 1995 and converted into a modern office block. By January 1996 another eleven staff had been appointed and the offices opened to the public. The Official opening was performed by Andrew Welsh MP in February 1996.

In February 1997 the Association more than doubled in size when we acquired 493 houses throughout Angus from Scottish Homes. This was a direct result of an overwhelming 91% of tenants in Arbroath, Brechin, Carnoustie, Forfar and Montrose voting in favour of our stock transfer proposals. This also added sheltered housing to our stock which was a whole new ball game!! It also gave us stock in Brechin and Forfar as well as Montrose and Arbroath and our existing rural housing.

From this time on things changed quickly and the Association took on a whole new perspective. Tenant Forums had been set up during the Stock Transfer bid process and some of these tenants then joined the Committee. Regeneration was high on the agenda. With the encouragement of Angus District Council, Strathairlie and Cliffburn in Arbroath were sizeable regeneration areas and involved environmental works as well as new build homes. With the financial help of Communities Scotland we employed a Community Development Worker to work with the Cliffburn Residents Association. With his help they raised £256,000 to build a Community Park. This involvement with tenants, and the wider Community role was quite new to us as a Committee of Management and we found that we needed training sessions to get us up to speed with everything we were now responsible for.

We had been trying to buy sites in Kirriemuir and after several years of negotiation our first development was opened on Tannage Brae in Kirriemuir in 1998. Since then we have built houses on several sites in Kirriemuir, and in the villages of Westmuir and Airlie to the west of Kirriemuir.

The Stock Transfer brought with it an increased maintenance programme, and in 1999 we increased our workload, our stock and our catchment area with the transfer of engagements of Caimridge Valley Housing Cooperative. This was a small Housing Cooperative in Mid Craigie , Dundee with seventy-eight houses, and it had been struggling to get enough Committee Members. The cooperative voted for Angus HA as their preferred partner. As well as the existing new houses in this development there were more phases planned for new build. We were now working with two Councils – Angus and Dundee, and a small satellite office was set up in one of the houses in the development.

Then a merger with Ormiston Peoples Cooperative in Whitfield Dundee in 2004 increased our role even more, bringing another 228 houses into management and the prospect of further development in Dundee. This gave us a permanent office in Dundee and the satellite in Mid Craigie reverted to a house for rent.

In 2007 Hazel Farquhar became our first tenant Chairman – appropriately a tenant from Auchmithie village! Also in 2007 we won Heritage Lottery funding to replace a Portakabin and build a new Lounge for the Sheltered Housing complex in Russell Square in Arbroath. This included the scheme office and a guest bedroom, as well as the communal laundry and lounge. We then converted the loft space into a meeting room for the Committee. New Disability Access laws rendered this redundant and we now have a ground floor Meeting Room in our office at 93 High Street, Arbroath.

Every change of Council or Government brought changes in the way funding was provided. Scottish Homes became Communities Scotland, then the SNP scrapped that and the Scottish Government now allocates housing development funding to Councils. We have to bid and compete for whatever small amount of funding might come our way, with grant ratios falling so low we were unable to continue developing new schemes.

During this process we lost our Development department, and at the time of writing, we are almost totally dependent on Section 75's as our only source of providing new homes. Even then, grant subsidies are not at the realistic levels they have been in the past, and private finance is more difficult and expensive to source.

We now have a total of 1,800 homes in management spread through all the towns and some of the villages in Angus. We employ thirty-five full time and six part time staff in offices in Arbroath and Dundee There are fourteen members on the Committee of Management, still made up of retired professionals, self-employed people and tenants and we still meet on Wednesday mornings. I am now the longest serving member of the Committee of Management and Secretary of a very different Association from the one I joined thirty-eight years ago.

What of the future? The good news is that currently there are several areas where the Association may have development opportunities in Angus and Dundee. Five units for rent in Kirriemuir; assessing the feasibility of developing in Monifieth; working with a builder to deliver six homes in Montrose and linking that with eight units for rent in Arbroath. Assessing the feasibility of development modules in tandem with Kingdom HA in Fife for homes in Dundee; and lobbying Dundee City Council regarding the site of Mid Craigie Primary School.

But it's all a far cry from the straggle of run down cottages in the village where this Housing Association began.

A draper and a fisherman . . .

Albyn Housing Society

*One of the earliest Highland based associations was Albyn Housing Society based in Invergordon. It is now at the forefront of innovation. **Donald Lockhart,** who was until recently the Development Manager tells the story of the early days and the commitment of the volunteer committee members.*

Donald Lockhart.
SFHA photo

In 1973, a group of local people including George 'Kelly' Kelman (whose draper's shop now features heavily in the mural adorning his former shop premises) and the redoubtable Jim Oag, former fisherman of Thrumster, met to form the Albyn Housing Society Ltd. The prospective Committee members who convened on that occasion could scarcely have imagined that, forty-two years later, Albyn, still uniquely retaining the *Society* suffix, would have developed into a large, diverse and successful housing association with nearly 3,000 homes in management across over sixty communities with, in addition, thousands of homes provided under the banner of Low Cost Home Ownership of which Albyn was an early and faithful champion.

They met in the gloomy, north-facing committee room of the Council Townhouse in High Street, Invergordon (later to be converted into homes for rent by Albyn's Development team) presided over by the severe (and one might be forgiven for thinking, judgmental) presence of a long-departed Provost of the town resplendent in a gilt frame and bedecked in the trappings of office. Here it was that the Adam Society of Edinburgh put together the putative Albyn Housing Society Ltd, an Industrial and Provident Society and registered with the Housing Corporation to provide the beginnings of a unique and lasting contribution to meeting the housing needs of the Highlands.

Invergordon was an interesting place to begin this work. The town with the insufficiently recognised naval history, scene of the last naval mutiny in 1931 and a place with natural advantages that contributed so much to the defence of the nation in two world wars both at sea and in the air.

By 1973, however, Invergordon's naval history was mostly behind it apart from the highly visible and ever-present oil tank farm which still today provides a reminder of its former role of fuelling the Atlantic fleet since the tanks first appeared in 1913. The tanks were later supplemented by a vast tunnel for 5.6 million gallons of oil storage dug out of the rock at Inchindown above Invergordon created to feed heavy fuel-oil the four miles to the Seabank oil depot and pier head by a system of pipelines, pump-houses and heaters. The destruction of Tank 13 in February 1941 in a Luftwaffe air-raid only contributed to the legacy of hydrocarbon pollution which housing developers and others have had to consider as a result of Invergordon's extraordinary military/industrial legacy.

By 1973, Invergordon had another string to its bow. The establishment in 1971 of the British Alcan (BACO) aluminium smelter at South Lodge changed the town of Invergordon in ways that even its role as a major naval base hadn't done. Conceived in the mid-sixties when, according to Harold Wilson in 1963, the future would be forged in '. . . the white heat of technology', the smelter would prove to be pivotal in the future of the town and of Albyn Housing Society Ltd. The depth of navigable water in the Cromarty Firth, so critical to the establishment of the naval base decades earlier proved essential for the delivery of colossal quantities of bauxite to produce aluminium which was going to be so important to Britain's industrial future.

As industrial intervention strategies go, it was not a success. Dogged by problems of unsustainable electricity supply contracts and remoteness from energy generation (for an industry that depended on vast supplies of affordable energy), changes in the world market in aluminium and operating losses, the smelter closed amid bitter recriminations in 1981.

The social economic and environmental legacy of the smelter, however, was significant with the industrial concern having imported many hundreds of workers and their families from the central belt of Scotland and elsewhere to build and run the plant and its ancillary operations. These new arrivals having established themselves in Invergordon mostly chose to remain living in homes provided for them by the newly-established Albyn Housing Society (and by the Scottish Special Housing Association) in South Lodge and Inverbreakie Drive. The impact of this movement of people was considerable. Until the relatively recent Large Scale Voluntary Transfer of local authority and SSHA homes to a new or existing housing association, Albyn had, more or less overnight, been established as the housing association with the single largest housing estate in Scotland. Effectively, from a standing start, Albyn had a management portfolio exceeding 400 homes, many tenants of which were now, following the precipitate closure of the smelter, out of work. Equally important, re-employment prospects were poor to non-existent having been imported from their own local areas as part of an over-ambitious attempt at industrial inward investment.

The problems for the early Albyn Housing Society didn't end there. Albyn at that time had no Development staff of its own, the new homes at Inverbreakie and South Lodge having been procured from Messrs. Taylor Woodrow. The timetable for the establishment of the plant and the workers needed to operate it meant that the emphasis was on housing that was cheap and quick to build. Many of the houses were constructed using a specification that scarcely suited the conditions of the Highlands of Scotland and a protracted dispute ensued before a settlement with Taylor Woodrow was agreed which allowed Albyn to make a start on bringing the homes up to an acceptable standard.

In due course, the Society appointed its own staff, at first operating from a vacant house in South Lodge to manage the not insubstantial task of managing Scotland's largest housing association estate. Chief amongst the new recruits was the formidable Colonel John Clark whose military background was well suited to the task of knocking this new organisation into shape, allowing it to find its feet and think about how its area of operation and remit might expand beyond the confines of Invergordon to other locations demonstrating housing need and where there was a job to be done.

Growth

By the mid-1980s, the growing staff of Albyn was added to by the appointment of Ian Chavasse as Development Officer (whom the author replaced in 1989) and the impetus to grow through development began to gather momentum. Working with various local authorities across the

Highland and funded largely by housing association grant from the Housing Corporation in Edinburgh where Albyn was forming relationships important to its future with Raymond Young and Coinneach Maclean, Proposals were initiated which would see the Society's portfolio of rented homes increase with projects in Golspie, Inverness, Wick and Thurso. The 1980s also saw the first tentative steps for Albyn Housing Society into the Low Cost Home Ownership (LCHO) market which was to become such a feature of its work in later years. Properties acquired from MacRae Builders in Scorguie and from Tullochs in Gordonville Road, Inverness represented the beginning of an effort which would affect many people's lives over the next three decades.

In the author's experience it is one of the most lasting and positive testimonies of the role of Albyn to hear the stories of people for whom the purchase of a shared ownership or shared equity property from Albyn proved the essential springboard for a better life after relationship breakdown, ill-health or business failure.

The increasingly Highland–wide approach of the early Committee of Management reacting to encouragement to extend their housing ambitions wider than just Invergordon, saw a real effort to recruit Committee members from across the Highlands to reflect that wider role and remit. This produced a fascinating cast of characters over many years who gave of their time, willingly and on a voluntary basis to what they saw as a worthy cause. It's no surprise that many of the most memorable came from and represented Caithness. One such was the remarkable Anderson Murray, a councillor from Wick who could secure the committee's full attention by the mere raising of a prodigious eyebrow. Anderson Murray was a man who had not come lately to serving his community or indeed his country. Serving with the RAF in War of 1939–1945 as a navigator, he once guided his fellow aircrew to safety from a flight over occupied Europe using only the stars, all navigation equipment having been rendered out of action by enemy fire. His driving style was as legendary as his wartime exploits once explaining to the author, tongue in cheek, that the reason that he and Jim Oag didn't travel together to meetings in Invergordon from Caithness was that Jim refused to be a passenger in his vehicle as 'he (Anderson) had a string of driving convictions as long as my arm'. The sentiment was entirely mutual – he equally shunned lifts from Jim Oag because of what he considered Jim's reckless driving style and excessive speed. Jim Oag himself was a founder member of the Committee of Management and only retired from that role in 2014 after forty years (including a spell as Chair of the organisation) of arguing the case for housing investment in Caithness and elsewhere and being constantly supportive of the work of the Development Team on whose efforts the success of the business was increasingly dependent.

Other notable characters to occupy seats around the committee table over the years included Heather Sheerin, founder of Sharon Leon, the successful carpet and flooring business in Inverness (also appointed to the Board of Scottish Homes, and chair of its Rural Committee), Dr. Alex Morrison a senior Health Board official and the Rev Allan MacArthur of Lochcarron to say nothing of the former Caithness head teacher, Mr. John Ross a genuinely nice man whose wife was the Mary Berry of Caithness and hugely welcoming in their home. The breadth and depth of knowledge and experience amongst the ranks of the Committee of Management was illustrated for the author by an occurrence at a public meeting in Lochcarron in the early 1990s. Utilising money from a fund created by the Howard Doris Company which operated the oil fabrication yard at Kishorn, a local group, the Strathcarron Project had conceived the creation of what was to become the Howard Doris Centre, an exemplar of good, local community provision – a mix of care services and housing provision. Indeed, in an act of innovative joined-up thinking, the proposal also provided a new space for the Lochcarron public library in a clever decision to ensure that integration of important local services could be possible to prevent the isolation of provision for older people.

This complex project involving more than half a dozen agencies was chaired by the late Rev Jackie Ross whose powerful advocacy of the needs of local elderly people was matched by the drive and enthusiasm of local GP Dr. David Murray and together, with the assistance of local authority professional expertise and project management and housing input including funding from Albyn Housing Society, a unique and valuable contribution to the life of this part of Wester Ross was established. The early days of the project were challenged by the problem that has faced most West Coast development projects before and since – where to build such a thing given the very challenging topography and local conditions. The answer, after much geo-technical and engineering investigation was to found at a site just above the shoreline at Millbrae, Church Street,

Lochcarron. The solution was far from straightforward. The land in question (from the evidence of seaweed frequently strewn across it) was susceptible to inundation by the high tide and an engineering solution was needed involving the importation of suitable material to raise the overall level of the site to create a building platform. In addition, further sea protection was necessary by constructing a rock-armoured bund. This proposed engineering solution was not accepted by all parties and a lively public meeting was called where Alan Cruden, a well-known Inverness-based Civil and Structural Engineer outlined his proposals to create a safe building platform which would be protected against any reasonably predictable sea conditions. The rock-armour bund proved a bone of contention with Jim Oag. It was Jim's opinion, from his wide experience of the sea conditions of the Pentland Firth, that a far more solid and substantial structure would be required in order to eliminate the risk to the resources and the reputation of the Society. Not so, countered Alan Cruden; the rock-armour was designed to absorb the energy of the sea rather than resist it completely and the suggestion of a solid concrete barrier such as Jim Oag was suggesting was inappropriate and more likely to lead to the apocalyptic outcome that Mr. Oag was predicting.

The intervention of Rev MacArthur was decisive. 'I was' he started with characteristic understatement 'a Meteorologist for thirty years, and I've lived here most of my life and I know something about the wind and tides in Lochcarron. Everything is going to be just fine.'

A meteorologist! Who knew?

The meeting closed five minutes later with a prayer and a firm instruction to the author to continue the work of developing the centre in line with Alan Cruden's proposals. The Howard Doris Centre was opened two years later by, the then, Lord Chancellor, Lord MacKay of Clashfern, and it was obvious to all concerned then as it is now that the facility would be valuable in sustaining and improving the life of the community which it serves. Reverend Allan Macarthur had an important role in furthering the progress of a vital social asset which offers dignity to its oldest and most respected members.

The late Marge Sieczkarek MBE was a committee member for many years and served the Committee well and with dedication and was particularly interested in the special projects that Albyn became involved in such as the development in 1990 of John Clark House, a dedicated

116

Howard Doris Centre.
Photo from Albyn HS

facility for the Homeless in Inverness. Marge's dedication to her community through interests in sport, music and remembrance of Inverness's connection with war in Europe through the City of Inverness Town-Twinning Committee was remarkable and properly honoured by H.M. the Queen. It seems highly likely to the author that Marge is equally remembered in St. Valery-en-Caux in Normandy, France such was her vivacity and particular brand of Invernesian charm. Even to a great age she never missed an Albyn AGM and one August evening in the Isobel Rhind Centre Marge Sieczkarek appeared late at the event during the Chairman's address, entered through the emergency exit, knocked over a stand or two with intruder alarms ringing while Reg King, with an unflappability borne of active service in the Paratroop Regiment, gamely carried on with his speech having turned off his hearing aids.

Reg King MBE's hearing was compromised by mortar fire on active service and served more than one period as Chairman of Albyn and carried a huge deal of respect from Committee, staff and tenants alike but he was far from deaf about the needs of the Highlands and its people. Unfailingly supportive of staff and very enthusiastic for the work of the Development team whose completed developments he was always very interested to visit, Reg saw the benefits of building new homes and constantly advocated that more could be done. He was particularly keen that funding agencies got the message that investment in affordable housing meant training places for young people and never missed an opportunity to make his point to the many housing ministers and other dignitaries that graced Albyn project opening with their presence.

Much has changed since 1973 when the original Albyn Committee sat for the first time; legislation, regulation and governance requirements have transformed the organisation and the same can be said for many other associations capable of tracing their history to the very beginnings of the voluntary housing movement in Scotland. What hasn't changed is the contribution made by people; selfless, public spirited individuals who are the hallmark of what makes the housing association movement what it is. It wasn't Major Repairs HAG or deficit funding which enabled Albyn to build a great housing brand and provide homes for thousands of families, it was the dedication of people like Jim Oag with his hilarious off-message conversations with Housing Ministers; like Marge Sieczkarek MBE, whose dedication to a range of causes was legendary; like Rev Allan MacArthur and Reg King, MBE whose quiet authority and good humour was so telling on so many occasions.

Housing is about bricks and mortar but only up to a point, it's more about people and communities; people who want to get involved because they feel they can make a difference contributing to the sustainable development of their communities. So it was with the early pioneers of Albyn Housing Society Ltd and many people right across the Highlands from Applecross to Auldearn and from Wick to Westercraigs have good reason to be grateful for their efforts.

Scotland's Heart

Rural Stirling Housing Association

Tony Teasdale.
Photo from Rural Stirling HA

Sitting at the heart of Scotland, much of it within easy commuting distance of both Glasgow and Edinburgh, Stirling Council area was one for which a housing association was one way of ensuring that affordable rented and low cost home ownership accommodation was available. **Rosemary Williams**, *a founder member of the association, and the current Director,* **Tony Teasdale**, *recount the early history of Rural Stirling Housing Association, setting out the challenges that faced the local authority and how the housing association was both encouraged and supported in its development by both the local authority and by Scottish Homes. Its story typifies that group of associations that were developed in the light of the 1990 Rural Policy.*

Rosemary Williams.
Photo from Rural Stirling HA

'*Stirling District has housing needs in its rural areas which are not being met. New houses need to be built, existing houses need to renovated, local people need to be involved.*'

These are the opening words of *The Case for a Rural Housing Association in Stirling District*, a report by Stirling District Council's then Housing Director, Steve Mason, in July 1989 which might be considered as the starting point for the formation of Rural Stirling Housing Association (RSHA). It succinctly set out the main issues and problems in relation to housing in the rural Stirling area and proposed the formation of a new local housing association, to be run by local people.

The area in question is that part of the Stirling Council area to the west and north of the M9, covering a total area of 850 square miles including a population of around 20,000 within around thirty settlements. It stretches as far as Killin and Tyndrum in the north, is bounded on the west by Loch Lomond and has a southern boundary stretching from Strathblane in the west to the outskirts of Stirling in the East. Callander, the largest settlement, sits roughly in the centre. The majority, northern part of the area falls within Loch Lomond and Trossachs National Park.

Following on from the Council's report things moved quickly, with support from both the Housing Department and Scottish Homes. Public meetings were held in September 1989 in Balfron and Callander, under the auspices of the respective Community Councils, to gauge interest in the establishment of a new housing association. The Balfron meeting in particular was very well attended and the proposal enthusiastically received. Steve Mason reported that a guest speaker, Brian Gegan then of Loreburn Housing Association, gave an inspirational speech. *'A rural Stirling housing association was not just a dream but becoming a reality!'* recalls Rosemary Williams.

Housing pressures and challenges in the rural Stirling area

The issues of concern within the Council report were outlined in more depth within *A Local Housing Market Analysis of West Stirlingshire* (Douglas Robertson and Sarah Heron, Stirling University, May 1990). This was commissioned by Scottish Homes as one of a series of similar studies from throughout rural Scotland, to help inform the development of its Rural Policy. This covered only the southern part of the rural Stirling area, closest to the urban settlements and most affected by commuting and housing pressures. It excluded Callander and the more remote rural areas to the north, where tourism was the mainstay of the economy, although some of the issues raised also applied there.

Key themes highlighted by the Housing Market Study included:

- A buoyant housing market, with the south west (Strathblane, Killearn, Balfron and Drymen) particularly influenced by the Glasgow market and

- Significant growth in new build supply for owner occupation in the 1980's but this very heavily focused on large (three or four bed) detached properties and a high propensity for these to be sold to incoming commuters and priced at upper end of the market.

On the other hand the Study found real challenges facing affordable housing supply within the area:

- A lower than average proportion of the overall stock in the West Stirling settlements was 'public sector' (Council/Scottish Homes or HA) – only 21% compared with 39% for Stirling District as a whole and just under 50% for Scotland.

- This in part due to a very significant loss of Council stock through RTB sales: 17.5 % of the total in these South West settlements between 1981 and 1989, and this particularly marked in Strathblane for example, where a reduction from 22% of all homes in 1981 to only 14% in 1989 was cited.

- No new Council homes had been built since 1983 and Housing Association activity was negligible and focused exclusively on sheltered and amenity housing (but even this type of accommodation was less prevalent than elsewhere).

- Issues regarding the range and quality of the Council stock:
  - Predominantly three and four bedroom with a significant under-supply of smaller homes given the high proportion of single people and couples on the housing list.
  - No Council housing to meet particular needs in the rural area, even for elderly people.
  - A relatively high proportion of pre-1945 and non-traditional house types – requiring substantial investment, with an uncertain timetable for this to take place – and evidence of tenant dissatisfaction as a result.

And the Study also described changes *within* the private sector that were adversely affecting the availability of homes to meet local needs:

- A very significant reduction in the private rented sector (from 7% down to 1%) and tied accommodation (from 11% to 1%) during these years.

- Forestry Commission properties being sold off and issues for Water Board employees on retirement.

- A high proportion (60% – 573 homes) of the Below Tolerable Standard (BTS) stock in Stirling was situated within the rural area.

- Serious issues for older owners – and no Care and Repair service being operated locally.

Against a background of projected population growth and general difficulties in accessing developable land the prognosis was not good. The latest Central Region Structure Plan had acknowledged the mismatch between supply and local needs and the requirement to build for 'local needs' throughout the rural area. However, in the absence of Council or housing association development activity there was no delivery mechanism in place. Builders were not keen to do low cost housing; the Council was no longer building and at that stage there was no housing association activity.

Building the organisation

In making its case for a rural housing association, the Council highlighted some of the opportunities that a new housing association would benefit from, including:

- Council land bank of sites
- Commitment of both the Council and Scottish Homes
- Strong Community Councils in key settlements and enthusiasm of local community for solving housing problems.
- A relatively buoyant economy.

And so the proposed remit for the locally based housing association became:

- To develop an understanding of housing needs and problems
- To build new homes which people on low wages can afford
- To acquire property for rehabilitation and/or conversion
- To provide agency services in the private sector to enable owners to improve their properties
- To operate Care and Repair services
- To raise funds from all sources to meet local housing needs
- To look into the possibilities of:
  - Leasing schemes

- Equity sharing
- Shared ownership
- Joint ventures with the District Council and private sector.

It was not simply about building a few homes, but creating a rural housing anchor organisation providing a variety of services – a Local Housing Agency.

After the initial September meetings follow up meetings were held in Aberfoyle in October and November 1989 to identify potential members of a Steering Group and to agree a brief for the procurement of a consultant to work with the steering group to take the proposal forward. Rosemary clearly remembers the start: '*Our first meeting was held in the Memorial Hall in Aberfoyle where we introduced ourselves and I recall the delighted enthusiasm of those present. However some doubts were also expressed – would a Housing Association in this rural area really be able to make a difference to people's lives by offering good quality rented accommodation?*'

The Council engaged a consultant to produce a *Plan of Priority Actions over three Years* which would define the organisational format, propose a constitution, identify financial viability within three years, and co-ordinate a Management Committee training programme. Preliminary meetings were held in Balfron and Callander and attended by nominated community councillors from the rural community councils. The appointed consultant, Evelyn Vernea, coordinated a training programme for the Group, in conjunction with representatives of Scottish Homes. The objectives during this period were to be able to meet the requirements of a Registered Housing Association and also to start to put together a viable programme of sites for development to be able to make the case for Grant funding to Scottish Homes. Meetings were attended by staff from the Council and Scottish Homes.

Steering Group members demonstrated real commitment to this process particularly given the geographical spread from Mugdock, near Strathblane to Tyndrum! All were volunteers with little experience of issues around the development and management of social housing. The training was difficult to organise, but worked!

David Frood (the other founding Member who is still on the Committee) recalls '*A vibrant group; excitement at making steps towards getting houses built to meet needs*'. Despite the group including a lot of strong characters and from very diverse backgrounds he remembers 'a *strong bond between the group members in those early days*'.

Registration was ultimately achieved in December 1990. The first shareholding members and Committee was spread throughout the area as follows: Jimmie Fraser (Balfron); George Watt (Gartmore); Mary Johnston (Aberfoyle); Dorothy Simpson (Balfron); John Fallon (Glenogle); Jim Milne (Fintry); David Frood (Blanefield); Rosemary Williams (Thornhill); Dr Mairi McColl (Killin); Derek Bean (Thornhill); William Johnstone (Aberfoyle); Connie Hare (Mugdock); Alistair Beaton (Kippen); Helen Scott (Gargunnock).

Many of this group were to be the bedrock of the Committee for many years to come, and supplied the Association's first four Chairs during the period up to 2007!

The first, post-Registration, meeting of the Association's Management Committee was held on 11 December 1990 in the Council Chambers, Callander and chaired by David Frood. The first Office Bearers were elected at this meeting, as follows:

Convener – Mary Johnston
Vice Convener – Jim Milne
Treasure – Derek Bean
Secretary – Connie Hare

Early meetings of the Committee alternated between Aberfoyle Memorial Hall and Callander. The early months were dominated by setting up the organisation. Development, Housing Management and Finance and General Purposes sub-Committees were

The opening of homes at Stirling Road Callander in 1992. Deborah Cunningham, the tenant (who still lives in the house) along with the Association's first Chair, Mary Johnston and Tom Begg, Scottish Homes Board Member.
Photo from Rural Stirling HA

established. The appointment of the first staff Member (Director) and lease of office, the ex-tourist Information centre at Leny Road, Callander. And lots of discussion regarding possible sites. Like other newly fledged associations with no assets at this time there was a reliance at this time on 'seedcorn' funding from Scottish Homes and other revenue funding (e.g. promotional Grant) from Stirling Council.

The official, public launch of the Association was on 14 June 1991 at the Golden Lion Hotel, Stirling. It had taken two years to get to this point from the original Council report.

Early development activity

The Association faced a number of challenges on the development front. Sandy Watson, Development Manager for the newly formed Scottish Homes Central Region office, was involved throughout the early years of the Steering Group and Association. He reports misgivings about whether a stand-alone Association could be a success, given:

- *Grant funding constraints* within the Central region at that time as:
  - the Regional programme was only really just getting off the ground and with a need to also fund the two other newly emerging associations – Forth Housing Association and Ochil View Housing Association
  - the relative priority of rural areas as opposed to big cities was only beginning to be raised through the new Rural Policy and had not yet been translated into a significant diversion of the national funding pot
- *Available sites:*
  - challenges in identifying viable sites that could be progressed within cost constraints – ransom strips a common problem
  - the relatively small numbers of homes that could be accommodated on potential sites
- *Income generation*
  - the pressing need for the Association was to build up a stock of rented homes as soon as possible to generate income

He reports though that this did not stop Scottish Homes from putting 'heart and soul' into supporting the endeavour.

There was a real interest and commitment amongst Committee Members to develop new homes and individuals would keenly identify sites. Members often had their own local preferences and in some cases land themselves to offer! Not all of these were viable but often required to be fully assessed.

The Council also continued to provide active support, lobbied for additional funding and also, critically, sold key sites to the Association from its land-bank.

There was, however, a need for the Association to be innovative and pragmatic to get the first homes built and meet needs. There was early site acquisition activity at Buchanan Street, Balfron and Willoughby Place, Callander followed by the purchase of a site in Strathyre. However, the Association's first completed development involved the acquisition in April 1992 of six flats off the shelf, purchased from a struggling builder at Lomond Court, Aberfoyle. The second, in August 1992 was a wholly shared ownership development of twelve units at Endrick Gardens, Balfron though an arrangement with a private developer.

The first new homes built at the Association's initiative and to its design were at Stirling Road/Campbell Court Callander, just over a year from the public launch. Developments at Buchanan Street, Balfron, Old Station Court, Strathyre and Mansefield, Tyndrum followed.

The Strathyre development was linked with environmental improvements to the centre of the village and the building of a new shop and

Rural Stirling Housing Association homes at Tyndrum.

involved close consultation with the community. It was regarded as a real success and gave the Management Committee some real confidence about what could be achieved. Part of the case for the Tyndrum development was the anticipated gold mine and related employment, in the area. Sadly this never quite materialised and is still an ongoing issue.

By 1995 the Association had achieved its 100th new home, with ten developments having been completed in eight settlements, including in Killin, Drymen and Gartmore.

Despite the fact that the Association's first Business Plan also referred to other activities envisaged within the Council's originally proposed remit – including: refurbishment of privately owned property; Care and Repair etc the main focus in these early years was very much on new build. From an early stage though discussions were ongoing with the Forestry Commission about possible transfer of its stock in the area. This was ultimately to lead to the acquisition and refurbishment of seven homes for rent with sitting tenants in 2000.

The Association now

Twenty-five years on from the Association's Registration much has been achieved. Over 600 affordable and relatively energy efficient homes – predominantly for rent – have been provided throughout the area.

This contribution has not just been about numbers. A range of house sizes and types, better reflecting current needs, have been built. Over 75% are one or two bedroomed. Many of our homes have been built to at least 'barrier free'/Housing for Varying Need standards of physical accessibility and we have many examples of homes built or adapted to meet individual needs. Our stock includes over 100 bungalows.

It's also been about how we operate. We have worked closely with communities over the assessment of housing needs and the mix and design of new homes. Also in respect of the use of Local Lettings Initiatives to ensure that, in pressured circumstances, priority has been afforded to those in housing need who need to remain in or move to the local area. These have often been critical in ensuring community support for new developments.

As a major landlord in the area we are achieving high standards of performance in our services to tenants. There is continuing high demand for our properties and high levels of tenant satisfaction are registered. We provide welfare rights, energy advice and other services to our tenants, aimed at helping them to sustain their tenancies.

We continue to have representation on our Management Committee from throughout the Rural Stirling area. As the only organisation with an exclusive focus on this area we aim to play a 'wider role', to help ensure the sustainability and inclusiveness of our communities. This has involved us in the provision of, or support for: environmental improvements; community facilities; projects around childcare and employment and training. We expect this role to grow in future

Challenges still remain however. Total Right to Buy losses in the area still outnumber the number of new homes that we (and latterly the Council) have been able to build and demand for new homes continue to far exceed supply. There are several villages in the most pressured south west area (Strathblane, Killearn and Fintry) where we have still not yet been able to build, although now hope to be able to do so in the near future. Owner occupation has become increasingly unaffordable to many on our lists and, as elsewhere, the only option is often high rent, insecure accommodation in the resurgent private rented sector.

We are fortunate to be one of the few smaller housing associations still developing new homes. In part this has been because of crucial additional funding support over the years from Stirling Council. We continue to work very closely with both the Council and the National Park Authority. Developing in this area remains difficult however, with limited – usually small scale and expensive – site availability. With most areas 'off-gas' there are challenges in ensuring that new (and existing homes) can achieve good standards of energy efficiency. We have recently established a non-charitable subsidiary – Venachar Ltd – to explore a wider and more innovative approach to affordable housing development and to work with private owners to help bring empty and other property into use at below market prices.

A final word from Rosemary Williams, looking back on over twenty-five year's involvement with the Association. *I'm very proud of what the Association has achieved. Volunteer Committee Members have contributed many thousands of hours of their time to ensure this could happen and there have been many difficult issues and decisions to deal with along the way. It's all worth it though when you see the very real impact – often transformational – on the lives of those housed, and the community as a whole.'*

Angus Housing Association. The opening of the Arbroath swimming pool housing project with George Mathieson, George Shepherd, Elizabeth Whitson and young swimmers.

Photo: Angus Housing Association

A happy tenant and her dog at Hamilton Green, Arbroath.

Photo: Angus Housing Association

Kishorn development by Albyn Housing Society.

Photo: Albyn Housing Society

Kinlochewe development by
Albyn Housing Society.

Photo: Albyn Housing Society

The completion of 50 houses in Springbank Road, Doune by Rural Stirling Housing Association. Tenant Sarah-Jane Walker and her children along with RSHA chair Margaret Vass and Housing Minister Margaret Burgess MSP.

Photo: Rural Stirling Housing Association

Rural Stirling Housing Association Development.

Photo: Rural Stirling Housing Association

Leadhills after refurbishment by Clydesdale Housing Association.

Photo: Clydesdale Housing Association

Happy tenants Mr & Mrs Roskilly of Lang Whang Court, Carnwath, Lanark.

Photo: Clydesdale Housing Association

A turbulent river runs through it . . .

Clydesdale Housing Association

*This story of Clydesdale HA is started by **Mary Taylor**, the founding secretary of the association in 1986. She gathered memories from others including council sponsor Lesley McInnes, former chair Bill Davidson, and George Tainsh the first project manager. Having moved to Stirling in 1990, Mary leaves it to **Wendy Hebard**, George's successor, to pick up the story from there, with **Joe Gorman**, the current Chief Executive bringing the story up to date. This story highlights the turbulence facing associations from their early days through their period of growth.*

As one of the most significant rivers in Scotland, the river Clyde gives the Clydesdale area its name. The river rises in the Southern Uplands and gathers in water from those pastoral hills before cutting down a series of falls and into the Clyde valley. The valley refers to a corridor running through the gorges in the south best known for the Falls of Clyde and New Lanark, and expanding out along ranks of tomato glasshouses and into what is now Strathclyde Park. Beyond the valley lies the industrial river of Lanarkshire between urban centres of Motherwell and Hamilton, Cambuslang, Dalmarnock, Bridgeton, Gorbals, Govan, and beyond the shipyards and docks out to the ocean. Cutting through Clydesdale is the M74 and the west coast line from Glasgow to London but most of us thunder through the magnificent landscape without stopping or thinking about housing.

Clydesdale is a term that barely exists today: it

applies to draught horses, which work in harnesses now mainly for show; and to a bank now owned by NAG (National Australia Group). But between 1974 and 1996 it was the name of a district council based around the county town of Lanark, and at the southern end of the regional council area of Strathclyde. The district bordered hills and forests to the south in Nithsdale, coal mining to the west in Cumnock and Doon, sheep and cattle farming to the east in Tweeddale with steel works to the north in Motherwell, and moorland towards Edinburgh.

It was one of fifty-six district councils which owned housing for rent and in the days when 'housing' meant council housing and little else. The stock was mostly terraced and shifting tenure under the right to buy. At that time councils were encouraged by the professional body (Institute of Housing now CIH) to think of themselves as having responsibilities beyond council housing: this included BTS (Below Tolerable Standard) housing, though some thought this was a matter for planning. There was a new CEO and with the appointment of a new Director of Housing, came a shift to a more enabling approach to housing. He brought in new staff in early 1986 to deal with aspects of service modernisation, all of whom eventually went on to lead organisations in housing and local government.

By 1980 I was living in New Lanark, in a house restored by my partner and me alongside other idealistic families keen to contribute to the renaissance of an industrial heritage based on former cotton mills powered by the waters of the Clyde. While my job as a housing professional was in tenement rehabilitation and urban regeneration in Govan, I also came home to house (and garden) restorations, on a smaller scale. Just as the house restorations came to an end and as I was preparing to go on maternity leave at the end of 1985, a letter arrived from the Housing Corporation in Scotland, inviting me to join a steering group for a housing association in Clydesdale as Raymond referred to on page 60, this was part of a plan for growth. No danger of boredom or wasting away at home!

The first meeting revealed the array of people invited, some of whom knew a lot about housing and some knew a lot about particular places and communities, some neither. Our steering group of nine included Bill, a teacher living in Tarbrax with his young family, Bob, a retired accountant from Lanark, another Bob – retired head of housing in the council, Ronald, a former council Chief Exec, two people from Leadhills, Elizabeth and George, a coal merchant. And we can add Jean from Lesmahagow, and

John from Carluke. And me, living in nearby New Lanark and on maternity leave from Elderpark HA in Glasgow. Although we started out as complete strangers to each other, some bonded quickly, united by the challenge of helping to improve housing conditions in the area. Some did not stay for long, others had more determination.

Our motivations were not all the same within the steering group and I don't recall that we ever took time to explore them – not what you did in those days. Bill who became our Chair, had plenty of patience, wisdom and determination which more than made up his limited experience. He was an experienced teacher, and maybe in need of a challenge. His own house was fine –but he reckons he liked a good cause! He had previously got involved in the Tarbrax community to take up issues about repairs to a road bridge into the village. I think others could see there was a problem with the villages and a need for new housing, which the council couldn't tackle itself. Some were more curious than committed. My own motivation (not least being on SFHA Council around that time) was to help evangelise what associations could do for local communities and translate my experience from Govan to Lanarkshire.

The organisers in the council confirmed to us that our priority was BTS housing, which they had identified concentrated in three diverse communities – first in the former lead mining village of Leadhills on the border with Nithsdale and thirty minutes off the M74; and at the other end of the district in two shale mining villages of Tarbrax and Woolfords, off the road between Carnwath on the way to Balerno, Edinburgh. I remember thinking: rural? really? But even Tarbrax and Woolfords were remote in terms of transport and access to services.

There was a potential opportunity to fund improvements to these houses via the Housing Corporation in Scotland (HCiS) if we could set up and register a housing association, based on the Glasgow model. For that we would need seven people willing to sign up, and be trained. The council had already commissioned research from University of Strathclyde and so the steering group had a technical survey and a social survey which showed the extent of dilapidations in the villages as well as the household composition and income profiles of residents, revealing many issues of health problems, grinding poverty, hidden homelessness and overcrowding.

Amongst the initial shared experiences in the group was that of visiting the villages to see conditions with our own eyes and it was an eye opener.

Each of the villages had a Wild West quality about it, in marked contrast to the ordered urban environments most of us occupied or knew. Some of the houses were empty and derelict, but standing in between and propping up other buildings which seemed to be lived in. It was all pretty ramshackle and reminded me a lot of rural Armagh where I knew people who resisted any modernisation. I should have understood that people who take on a remote property in poor condition will hang on to it, however awful it may be, because it may be all they have.

Among the first tasks of the steering group included communicating with residents about the scope for improvement. Many of us remember particular occasions quite vividly and consistently. Bill recalls it starting with a dramatic meeting in Woolfords hall one evening. The hall was a green hut and a local woman who shall remain nameless 'strutted up and down' passing judgement on the shortcomings of the association's proposals, presenting herself as saviour of the *status quo*. And there was a memorable meeting in Leadhills one Friday evening shortly after. On our way to the meeting (me with baby in tow), we were intercepted by allies from the community council saying the meeting had been hijacked by people from Woolfords. We decided to continue, in spite of advice to the contrary, and we walked into the Brigadoon café to answer questions, and dispel rumours about state interference by the association. The weirdest allegation was that Bill was picking up £25,000 to chair the association! In 1986!! We left the meeting after lengthy heated argument, and though not everyone was happy, we did change some minds, not least due to our courage in running the gauntlet, and for turning up to face the opposition.

Local hostility to our proposals took a toll on everyone in different ways. Some abandoned the steering group perhaps as a lost cause. And Bill and family moved away from Tarbrax to be nearer Lanark. Bill remembers long phone calls with Lesley, with me and other office bearers as we relied on each other for mutual support in those early days. He reminds me that I said I had never come across anything like this before – after years in east end of Glasgow and in Govan. I remember wondering what on earth we were doing spending time trying to improve conditions when people wanted nothing to do with us. And by then we began to suspect that while the council wanted the BTS problem solved, the HCiS was not convinced about funding the association to rehabilitate housing in these villages. Lesley too remembers wondering how it could ever work, since everywhere else people in poor housing were crying out for support to improve, not resistant to 'interference'.

For me it was shocking to see the desperately poor living conditions, particularly in Leadhills. The constraints of rehab within the existing shell were horrendous. The buildings had been randomly assembled by miners who'd gone there seeking their fortune from lead. They built shelter with whatever materials which were to hand – rubble, tree trunks, pick axe handles, so the structures were precarious, unpredictable. The costs of rehab were beyond anything experienced in the cities. At £90,000 for a one bedroom house (in 1990 prices), it would undoubtedly have been cheaper to knock down and start again to build to modern space and energy standards but the commitments made to residents were about preserving what could be preserved. As important, the improvement grants paid to owners under the Housing Action Area legislation would not have been available and a whole new route for the regeneration project would have had to be found. To have raised any argument at the start about the economic cost would have produced a riot. Had we known the costs at the start, projects might never have got off the ground.

Looking back maybe the hardest part in the early days was just getting the facts across to residents – we had to keep an eye on the local press to be able to counter negative publicity. With hindsight, we should have sought advice on communications and PR but we didn't know that at the time. It felt like we were pioneers in Wild West conditions.

If the reception from residents was poor, it wasn't that we could take for granted consistent support from the powers that be. There was division within the council between senior officers, and between the council and HCiS over the right thing to do – rehab in the villages or new build somewhere else. Some in the council were obstructive and indeed after Lesley left, Bill resigned, because lack of support from the council for the association tipped the balance for him in favour of spending more time at home. He had come to the conclusion that the association had to develop beyond the villages in order to make it viable, which is why new build developments were later pursued in larger settlements, Carluke and Lesmahagow.

Lesley was our council sponsor and main source of staffing support until Thenew Housing Association was engaged to provide agency services. She thought new build would be the answer, not rehab and that this was an unresolved tension within early committee discussions. And it turned out, the funders also thought new build might be a better solution and that actually the national associations could take that on. By 1987/88 it was an issue for Scottish Homes as to whether to register more associations, who would then compete for funding. That all went to the heart of whether a local association could or should get off the ground. And that came back to the BTS problem for the council and the hunger to access resources not available to the council itself.

During the maelstrom of discussions the steering group persevered with training towards registration, supported by Thenew HA. We eventually managed to secure registration in 1987. By then there were proposals to separate the HCiS from the Housing Corporation (and form Scottish Homes). The scope of rehab work was clearer as was the commitment to it, but new build had firmly become part of the mix.

We took on our own offices on the High Street, Lanark, and in May 1988 secured the appointment of a member of staff, George Tainsh, who joined the association from Hillcrest. Not long after, he was joined by Jane Guthrie from nearby Carluke. Budgets were tight, so tight there wasn't a chair nor a desk, nor even a phone in the office. George queried the lack of a phone on his first day and had to justify why a phone would help him do his job . . . As he recalls, every penny would be a prisoner.

By the end of the first full year of operation, we had acquired rows of sub-tolerable housing but our one tenant was in arrears. And the financial regime for associations was about to change with the introduction of private finance. So things could only get better. Meanwhile George found alternative employment with newly-formed Scottish Homes, where he moved after eighteen months at Clydesdale, believing that the right ingredients were not in place to support the existence of the association. I was moving on myself around the same time, to live in Stirling with my young family. But a core of the committee kept going, attracted new members and the association advertised again and secured Wendy Hebard who started in 1989 and stayed for the best part of ten years. She now takes up the story.

The First Director's story

My first encounter with the Committee was at my interview for the post of Project Manager in Lanark one sunny Saturday in September 1989. My overwhelming impression was of the enthusiasm and commitment of those I met. I had applied for the job of Project Manager because I was interested in rural housing issues and also in need of a change after twelve years with Edinburgh District Council. I had undertaken a study of rural housing while studying part-time at Glasgow University for my professional housing qualification. As a development officer at heart, I was excited by the challenge and I was not to be disappointed.

As I was soon to discover, a lot had been achieved in the two years before I came on the scene, laying the foundations for the growth and development of the Association over the years and making my job easier too. Five houses in Tarbrax had been modernised and eleven more were due for completion in Leadhills. The staff of the Association was about to grow from one to three: George Tainsh, my predecessor, had left a month before, Jane Guthrie had been providing admin support for a year already, while Peter Kane started as the first housing officer on the same day as me, 16 October 1989.

Meetings were all held in the evenings and well attended. Bill Davidson was still in the chair with Bob Westworth, Mary Taylor, John Wilson and David Egginton as office bearers. There were members from Leadhills and from other areas too. Women were always in the minority, something that we tried to alter over the years, but it was a slow process. The first woman to chair the association, Jean Ramage, was elected after I left.

A few weeks after I started we had our first 'official opening' in Leadhills on a snowy December day. I was to learn very quickly the importance to the association of such opening ceremonies to mark its progress and publicise its achievements. In this and so much else, the committee was the driving force and they turned out in numbers on the day, despite the bad weather. We all scrunched down Symington Street to look at the newly-refurbished cottages and to watch Sir James Mellon, chairman of Scottish Homes, present Mrs Robb, one of the residents, with a painting of the street. We then returned to the Hopetoun Arms, the hotel and lodge belonging to the landowners Hopetoun Estates, for refreshments and to warm up.

Clydesdale committee at Leadhills opening.
Photo from Clydesdale HA

What I wasn't to know until later was that this was also a relatively good time for development funds for housing associations. Looking back I am surprised at how much we got as annual capital allocations; this grew over the years until in my last year, 1999/2000, when we were awarded over £2.5m in housing association grant. With loan funds from the banks, who came to appreciate that housing association developments provided them with good business, the association was able to grow to providing nearly 400 homes in the first ten years.

Initially, the development work was as part of Clydesdale District Council's Housing Actions Area programme. The houses were renovated with grants from the Scottish Office through the council for the privately-owned houses and Housing Association Grant (HAG) for the CHA houses, whilst the Association acted as agent for the council in return for co-ordination fees. Within the action areas, the association had acquired approximately two thirds of the unimproved properties to be let to those its waiting lists, whilst it renovated the remaining houses for their owners.

Once the programme shifted to mostly new build, from 1990, the Association was awarded HAG funding through an annual programme agreement with Scottish Homes. This required periodic meetings with Scottish Homes, first in East Kilbride and later in Hamilton. The Chair and I would take our plans and budgets to the Scottish Homes offices. In the early years, these meetings were quite stressful because we were under pressure in number of ways, to work with less HAG, to justify and deliver the projects we had put into the programme, to achieve the HAG target by the year-end and to put homes on the ground.

Then there was the question of surpluses. Scottish Homes wanted us to build up surpluses, in part to demonstrate to them that Clydesdale HA was a viable organisation and we did too, for the long-term security of the organisation. But that was a balancing act: if the surpluses reached a certain level, Scottish Homes could require the money to be put towards development schemes to reduce the HAG level, instead of protecting the association's viability.

Those pressures did abate over time. And generally the relationship between us and the Scottish Homes staff seemed to become more of a partnership, as they became more confident in what we could do and they recognised that they needed us to achieve their own targets. As their budget grew, Scottish Homes needed associations that could spend money reliably and make use of extra funds if they were heading for an underspend towards the year-end.

However, some tensions did not get resolved, not in my time anyway. There was always a downward pressure on costs but particularly on consultants' fees. I argued long and hard that we got fantastic value from our consultants. We relied on them a great deal, for instance in the early stages of development projects, when we needed them to work up a scheme but when fees for feasibility studies were not generally funded. Targeting consultants' fees in this way risked undermining the essential working relationships with consultants needed to produce high quality homes.

Clydesdale District Council was the other main partner in establishing the Association and working in the Housing Action Areas, and later in finding sites for our new build developments. Their local plan identified potential housing development sites in each settlement. In the rural parts of the District this was particularly helpful because good sites were scarce. It also helped at the planning stage because it meant that the land or property was already designated for housing.

The Council also sold sites it owned to the association. Thus CHA secured the site for the first new-build in Carluke from the Council and went on to acquire sites from them in Lesmahagow and Lanark for several more developments. Other sites were acquired from private owners. For example, in Abington, we acquired a disused filling station and in Kirkfieldbank, an old hotel building and land around it.

The relationship with Clydesdale District Council was nevertheless not an easy one. Under Margaret Thatcher and her successors, the government supported housing associations in preference to local authorities and poured large amount of public funding into the Housing Corporation and then Scottish Homes to fund their activities. Despite this public funding and their social housing role, housing associations were often labelled as 'private'. Clydesdale HA was viewed by some as depriving the Council of its funds and its housing development role, while leaving it with the responsibility for housing homeless and vulnerable people. Understanding this didn't necessarily make our meetings any easier.

These were not the only challenges. Land acquisitions could be delayed. In North Back Road, Biggar, rights to a drying green in the middle of the site had to be extinguished before the acquisition could be completed. Costs could be increased by work to the site: the site in Abington, now Hunter's Court, had fuel storage tanks and contamination from its previous use that had to be removed. We were helped enormously in the many property transactions by our solicitor, Gail Baker, whose thorough work at every stage and sound advice protected the Association's interests very well. Contracts were secured by competitive tender for a number of years with generally good results, although there were problems with one or two contractors. In the mid-nineties, pressure was on housing associations to use 'design and build' as a procurement route. There were concerns that in this form of contract, the client had less control over the design as the contractor provided the design service. As an early experience of this form of contract, CHA was fortunate to develop a good working relationship with a well-established local firm, Tinto Construction. They built two large mixed developments of good quality houses in Symington and Carnwath, with us having a large say in the design.

Finance was always a critical issue. Our annual allocation of HAG of about £1m in the early nineties, jumped to over £2.5m in 1994, but there was pressure on the HAG rate, which dropped from over 90% to about 70% over the ten years. Like others, we achieved this in part by introducing an element of 'shared ownership' into some developments. From about 1994 an element of Low Cost Home Ownership (LCHO) houses was included in most developments. CHA borrowed some funds from Scottish Homes in the early days to complement the HAG element before loans could be secured from private sources. They had very high interest rates so were redeemed later for private loans at much lower rates. Relationships with the bank lenders were generally quite good.

CHA bid for Scottish Homes Clydesdale stock, when it became available to buy in the early nineties, in an attempt to increase our stock and achieve economies of scale more quickly than just by building. This bid was a costly exercise, financially with added direct costs, and in the time and energy of staff and committee. At the height of the campaign in July 1997, we set up a trailer in Coalburn as a base for canvassing residents. It was a huge effort but the committee volunteers were undeterred. In spite of these efforts, the transfer was rejected by a majority of tenants, hostile to the idea of transfer to what they perceived as a 'private' landlord. It was a depressing outcome but much later the transfer of houses in Rigside and other areas went ahead successfully. Regarding community support, the Association had mixed fortunes in Tarbrax, Woolfords and Leadhills, as related earlier. Despite the success of the Symington Street improvements in Leadhills, the local community didn't seem concerned when Scottish Homes would not fund a second phase after many months of work, arguably reflecting the long-standing mixed views of what the Association was doing in the village and a level of residual resistance, if not actual hostility. However, I don't recall hostility to any of our development proposals elsewhere.

Although CHA was designated as 'community-based', it wasn't really, because we were operating over a wide area in many different communities with few or no links. For such a small organisation it would have been difficult to spend a lot of time building links in the different areas, but I was always bothered about this. It's great to know that has been achieved under Joe Gorman.

As the association grew, it was a relief to employ more staff to manage the increasing numbers of houses, particularly after so many project completions with the growth in grant from Scottish Homes during the 1990s. And taking on a full-time development officer in late 1993 proved timely to exploit this sharply increased development funding. In 1992, the association set up and managed a 'care and repair' service with John Gold as manager and funded by the Council and the Lottery in the first year. After some ten years it became a separate organisation, Care and Repair in South Lanarkshire, and continues to provide service to elderly local people from a nearby office.

Following the move to much more spacious office in North Vennel in 1993, in due course we invested in a better computer system and later, housing management and accounting systems. For such a small organisation, the administrative burden was disproportionately great, from allocations, rent accounting and repairs management, to grant applications and annual returns, plus the dreaded periodic 'monitoring' by Scottish Homes. Pressure was on too to embark on such things as lifecycle costing of repairs and to put in place policies about every aspect of what the association did.

The organisation would not have been set up or thrived without Committee members being 'hands-on' and taking a large share of the burden in the early years. In later years, they continued to serve the association through the various committees that were set up. Clydesdale HA was lucky too with the various consultants it used in the early years for development and finance assistance, such as Thenew and Cube housing associations.

In turn, it was the high level of commitment of the staff over the following years that ensured the success of Clydesdale HA. In my time there, the organisation was so fortunate to recruit people who were prepared to stay and to grow with the organisation: Jane Guthrie, who is still there as the Depute Chief Executive now, Joyce Watson, Vicky McGilvary, Paul Agnew, Jan Andersen, Eileen Wilson, who came just as I was leaving, and others, Peter Kane, Stuart Meikle, Fiona Imlach, who were not there so long but nevertheless contributed a great deal. I understand that this kind of commitment and growth has continued in the years since I left.

This stable staff team helped to forge good relations with the Clydesdale tenants from the early years and as the association grew. Unlike many housing associations, Clydesdale staff got to know the tenants, who very often came to feel part of the organisation and in turn for some, able to contribute to its success, whether by joining the committee or being part of a local tenant group or attending the AGM.

My last encounter with Clydesdale Housing Association, on the day I finally cleared my desk and handed in my keys, was at the AGM in September 1999. As ever, the formal business was followed by the quiz! The room was filled with staff, committee members and tenants, some I knew and some who were new to me. It was great fun and it was a great way to say goodbye and to hand over to Joe Gorman, who now finishes the story.

Mature by 2015

Clydesdale HA has built or improved around 750 properties for rent and over eighty homes for low cost home ownership. These are spread across thirty-six projects in fifteen towns and villages throughout rural South Lanarkshire acquired or developed since 1987. This is the result of over £40m investment, funded through public subsidy and private borrowing by CHA.

In 2002 and 2003 Clydesdale HA successfully competed against much larger RSLs to secure the majority support of 170 then Scottish Homes tenants to become their preferred landlord. Ten years after the initial attempt, Clydesdale had been able to build a reputation, and trust and support among local people. CHA has since invested in the transferred homes in Carluke, Kirkmuirhill, Lanark and Rigside.

In the nineties, tenants were either selected from the Association's own waiting list or were nominated by the Clydesdale District Council, and later South Lanarkshire Council. The Council was entitled to make nominations for 50% of the lets.

CHA collected some demographic information about its tenants in March 2014. In terms of age & gender CHA houses people across the spectrum of age from eighteen to over seventy-five, though the majority is bunched in the middle between thirty-five and seventy-five. There are slightly more men than women in the fifty-five+ age group but other age groups are balanced. Almost half of all tenants are single people, slightly more among the over sixties. About a third of all tenants are over sixty and coming up for a quarter are families with children. Around one in three households is retired, one in four is in work, and one in five are long term sick. One in twenty is unemployed, one in eight is looking after family.

The turnover of stock in Clydesdale is a steady 10% – 11% in recent years, which is about average and works out at about 75 vacancies a year. As a member of the South Lanarkshire Common Housing Register (Homefinder) CHA has approximately 3,350 applicants registered for its properties which equates to over forty applicants for every vacancy, on average. Although demand remains particularly strong for the rural centres of Biggar, Carluke and Lanark, it is the more remote rural locations and larger properties which are less popular and require additional marketing and imagination to maintain demand.

CHA charges rents typically lower than most rural associations at £64 a week for a two apartment (one bedroom) ranging up to £85 for a five apartment (four bedroom).

Today CHA is chaired by Iain Cochrane, with an impressive Management Committee. The knowledge, experience and professionalism of the committee isn't surprising given that it includes tenant activists, a former local authority finance director, a retired senior housing professional, a former health centre manager, a post office manager, a retired publisher and a local businessman.

A staff team of thirteen employees work across four departments: Housing Management, Technical, Finance and Corporate Services. Clydesdale supports staff learning and development and has supported staff with studies resulting in a wide range of qualifications being achieved across different levels. The staff team is led by Joe Gorman, Chief Executive. Staff work hard to maintain an informal environment with an emphasis on collaborative working. Managers aim to enable staff in pursuit of better service provision delivered in the way tenants enjoy, friendly and approachable.

CHA tenants and residents have established their own organisation and local groups. Former Chair Jean Ramage, is Clydesdale's longest serving Committee member, with over twenty years' voluntary service. A lifelong community volunteer, Jean was an early leader in the development of Clydesdale's Tenants' and Residents' Group, the current chair of which (Jeanette Arneil) is Chair of the East Dumbartonshire and Lanarkshire Regional Tenant Network – a forum that enables better communication and consultation between social housing tenants and the Scottish Government.

The Clydesdale Tenants' and Residents' Group was constituted in 2006 on the back of a tenant steering group. The well attended CTRG meets monthly in Clydesdale's offices and has tackled issues such as anti-social behaviour taken on reviews of service charges and reactive repairs. More recently, the CTRG has played a vital role in developing the content and format of the Annual Return on the Charter Report, which CHA makes annually to the regulator.

Clydesdale established tenant engagement originally through surgery and outreach work, however, demand for this decreased as mobile communication has become more prevalent. CHA is currently in the process of forming a tenant scrutiny panel and has applied to participate in the Tenant Information Service's Scrutiny Approved Accreditation Model.

The association publishes a newsletter 'You Spoke, We Listened'. We survey tenants and share with them the results about satisfaction compared with their priorities and standard reporting requirements. We show changes relative to last year and what we have done to address concerns. This helps to inform the dialogue between the association and tenants about service quality and value for money.

Clydesdale recently embarked on developing proposals for new office accommodation. And we are assessing need and demand for an integrated community hub facility within Lanark as part of this project. Local voluntary and charitable organisations have expressed strong interest in partnership working that would offer more comprehensive services and support to Clydesdale's tenants, and the wider community, under one roof.

Our houses meet existing standards (SHQS) but with over 25% of existing housing located in 'off gas grid' areas, achieving new energy efficiency standards (EESSH) will be a major challenge for Clydesdale. We have an options appraisal underway in 2015 to develop an investment strategy to meet those standards and to make it more affordable for tenants to heat and light their homes.

People who already live in most remote rural locations love the tranquility, sense of community and even the isolation that that brings. However, the very remoteness of these villages requires us to be effective in marketing any vacancies there, but there is demand. We think that our existing social housing in these areas has a future.

Our last new build development was completed in October 2012 with thirty-six homes for rent in Biggar. Although CHA is still registered as an active developer with South Lanarkshire Council, current grant and subsidy levels and the risks associated with new projects under existing procedures has deterred Clydesdale from pursuing any new projects recently. That may change with subsidy arrangements under review, but until the risk profile improves we will focus on managing what we have.

Leadhills.
Photo from Clydesdale HA

The Bunker Sisters
and the Bowling Boatmen . . .

The early days of Care and Repair

Although housing associations are best known for building and letting homes, one of the most important roles that many have played is that of helping older and disabled people to remain in their own home. The Care and Repair programme, as it became known, has been a life line for many. **Neil Clapperton**, *the Chief Executive of Grampian Housing Association remembers the early days of Care and Repair.*

Neil Clapperton.
Photo from Grampian HA

The history of it matters less than the fact that it happened at all. But revisiting the reason for Care and Repair does help understand the thinking behind it. If you go back far enough, my story starts with the failure of the private housing sector a century ago. Any student of housing history knows that this led to many interventions: Wheatley and the other housing Acts that pushed the rapid expansion of council housing, slum clearance and the mass demolition of communities, the late seventies rise of rehabilitation, housing action areas and the birth of community housing associations. Some were rightly celebrated; other outcomes were more qualified but the blunt and sometimes brutal ways in which governments, local and national, dealt with the stubborn and extreme problems of private renting and ownership eventually became victims of their own success. It appeared that absolute poverty of quality in the open market, as defined by measures such as 'Below Tolerable Standard' or BTS and exemplified by pre-1919 tenemental slums, was by 1990 a niche problem, overtaken in political terms by the challenges posed by council slums and community care.

But that mass success was also a foil for emerging problems, ones that the blunt tools of previous generations were wholly inadequate to deal with. Pepper potted across both rural and urban communities were people renting privately or living as home owners in property that was not fit for their needs. This was often due to the physical conditions they lived in, but as important were their disabilities, old age, or poor mental health, combined in many cases with an inability to help themselves because of their condition and their poverty. There were council grants but they required a level of knowledge, confidence and engagement that was just not there. It was a passive service in face of a muscular problem. And it was no longer about some absolute definition of what was tolerable to society but about individual needs and dignity.

The early days of Care and Repair were rooted in pioneering work in Scotland by charities like Age Concern and Shelter and the emerging network of rural housing associations. Those associations provided a dependable base for many of the new Care and Repair services, bringing with their organisational strength, an expertise in development, special needs and community engagement. The associations also brought a scale that allowed mistakes to be made and lessons to be learnt. But the two belonged, siblings representing different aspects of the zeitgeist. Associations had also emerged as a more human solution to housing problems and were complementary or perhaps even an antidote to big government interventions.

In that more enlightened and radical time, Scotland had a rural housing policy and a growing understanding of the problems of remote and island areas, and of the importance and complexity of community care in all places. Unfortunately the understanding was not universal and there were local authorities who didn't appreciate the importance of flexibility and generosity. It's only with a lot of hindsight that I know how lucky I was when I left the comparative order of the grants department in Edinburgh to start up a new Care and Repair service in Dumbarton District Council, a local authority that no longer exists but was in its time willing to make policy work for ordinary people and change old habits. Others like Castlehill Housing Association's Care and Repair service in the North East struggled with limited resources in the early years, where grants were severely limited and most work required extensive charitable fund raising.

Dumbarton and Clyde Care and Repair was hosted in its infancy by Dunbritton Housing Association, a commitment that was made even before it had houses to rent. Like all its peers Dumbarton and Clyde was about case work and the most extreme cases were truly rural, even remote, but also sometimes found on the fringes of cities and more urban areas, where the proximity to well-developed public services and modernity only stood to emphasise how awful living conditions were for those households. In Garelochhead, a village a few miles from the splendour of Helensburgh and closer still to the berthing place for the UK's most sophisticated weaponry, I found a young single mother with infants renting a derelict basement that looked like it had just stepped out of Edwin Chadwick's report on Victorian slums, so awful was the dampness and lack of sanitation and services. As Care and Repair grew, these eye-popping extremes were found across the nation. Nine miles from the most affluent city in Scotland one Care and Repair Officer found a woman cooking on an open fire, with no running hot water, with an outside washhouse and a derelict outside WC, in the mid-1990s.

But getting excited about the prurient detail misses the uniqueness of Care and Repair. When I was being interviewed for the job, one question came up time and time again: what would you do if you saw someone living in appalling conditions and they didn't want to move, or do what you thought was best for them, even when it threatened their own health. I trotted out something about patience and respect for their wishes, but was still thinking about the statutory standards we were all supposed to be trying to achieve. But that respect was an iron principle and it rapidly took over. In some cases you felt as though you were colluding in something wrong whilst absolutely doing the right thing.

My first contact with one of the most amazing examples of that principle came a matter of months after I'd started, in the early autumn. I had been getting a stream of referrals from the Council from the start, the more intractable cases, and the ones that the grants team struggled to find a solution to. On this day I was given an address and a name and wished all the luck in the world. The information was minimal: two sisters of pension age, an address in Kilcreggan. Their house was 'Below the Tolerable Standard' but it didn't look like grants could help.

I can't remember all the detail; it was over twenty years ago and I may have got some aspects of their story wrong. I have given them new names; in part because I'm not entirely sure of what is memory and what has been repackaged over the years. What I am confident of is the fundamental truth of their situation and the role of Care and Repair. But despite the vagueness, so much of the experience is still with me, even the weather on the first day. It was a glorious day. Sunshine was pushing through the trees that lined the loch and warming my skin. I'd not long learned to drive and this was my first trip down the Rosneath Peninsula.

The road up the coast from Dumbarton is pretty but as it twists up towards Garelochhead and then runs back down the loch, you realise how magnificent and quirky this part of Argyll can be. The route was marked out by Faslane Peace Camp with its eclectic assortment of caravans, tents and banners. At the top of the loch sat a house that looked, with its 1960s concrete brutal architecture, like a miniature Bond villain's retreat. All around were views that illustrated some long forgotten geography lesson on glacial valleys. The road itself was a source of constant surprise. For long stretches there was only a narrow strip of trees and grass between the tarmac and the water and I had been told to be careful driving as a council employee had recently sent his car straight into the Loch on a tight bend.

When I came to Kilcreggan, I was lost. The village only has one street, two at a stretch, so it took considerable lack of direction to be that confused. I consulted the reference address I had been given. It was a Gaelic place name, then Shore Road. I was pointed back the way I came and found a narrow lane passing down towards the Loch itself. Single track and without signs or much in the way of passing places, I managed to drive to the end and a hamlet called Portkil but couldn't see any building that might pass the description of their home, below tolerable standard or no. There were a couple of old World War pill boxes along the shore line but nothing else.

At Portkil the road turns away from the sea and runs up hill. On either side were buildings, some lived in judging by the gardens and curtains, but none answering to the name given. I got back into the car and turned around. On the way back I passed one pill box that had clearly had some work done to it. The next one had a rough hedge screening it from the road and a garden gate I had missed on the way up. I stopped and let myself into the garden. There were some items of flotsam garnishing the flowerbeds and there was something that looked like a lawn, cut recently and it was tidy and loved. I walked around to get a better look and approached the building from the sea. On the right side it consisted of a small brick structure with a flat roof and one window, glazed, with a steel frame. There was an entrance and a connecting passage that linked this red-brown brick shed with a massive concrete pill box on the left. To call it a pill box is to do it a disservice. It was a gun emplacement, squat, hunkering down into the landscape, the slot where the gun would have sat, narrow and wide enough to allow a sweep of fire across the loch, where it met the Clyde. It was crudely and amateurishly glazed with bits of marine ply and other useful wood, and a number of sheets of single glazing working at angles around the curve of the aperture. To the left and behind the emplacement was a low concrete blockhouse, again with a flat roof.

I knocked and an old lady of impeccable and slight appearance asked me in, and introduced herself as Margaret. She wore an old fashion dress, flowery and too light for the conditions but topped by a cardigan. I was welcomed into her kitchen, which was the brick shed. It was remarkably spacious inside, had a sink, an electric cooker, and a standalone plywood 1950's utility kitchen dresser, tall and narrow with a fold down work surface. By the window sat a covered table and two chairs. I was offered a seat and a cup of tea. We were joined by her sister, Connie, who was wearing working gear, an orange boiler suit. They were quite open about their circumstances. They had nothing but their unconventional home, and the state pension, and no savings to speak of. Although both had spent much of their youth in Kilcreggan, Connie's connection with the village was strongest, having been a baby sitter for most of the recent generations. With no family to help, and only having each other, they had no intention of moving. I checked their benefits. It was a given for Care and Repair that many of the clients were not getting the help they were entitled to. Any improvement in their circumstances could unlock funding possibilities, but their problem was that their health was good. I asked them to help me fill in some forms and give me some background, to which they responded with great patience and good humour.

So what was the 'house' like? Connie in particular was proud of their achievement and had lived there continuously since the 1950's, shortly after the base had been decommissioned in 1948. She knew its history. The battery was actually built in 1900 and was part of a more widespread military establishment in the Peninsula used by both the British Navy in the First World War and the US Navy during the Second. The brick kitchen had been the external magazine, separated from the gun to ensure that it couldn't be blown up by its own munitions. The space in between had been filled in by Connie using timber partitions with materials borrowed from people in the village or washed up on the shore. In this connecting piece between the magazine-kitchen and the blockhouse and emplacement she'd recently built in a small cubicle with an electric shower. They had existed without a bathroom but there was an internal toilet at least. The block house provided space enough for two bedrooms. The curved front slit with glorious views over the Clyde and Gare Loch was their living room window. When they had moved in their mother had paid for a chimney to be built that allowed an open fire to one side of the room. It had sanitation of sorts, because this had been provided along the road to the base along with electricity and teed off to the bunkers. They struggled with heating the building and every year Connie had to take a ladder onto the roof and apply patches of felt and hot bitumen to seal the inevitable leaks.

I asked them how they had come to live there. They were so open, telling me that when they were younger, as children, before the war, their family had lived in Greenock and their father had been a salesman. He had died young and left them penniless and facing destitution. Their saw the possibility of buying one of the bunkers because they were going cheap and could be adapted to live in. It wasn't unusual to find the ex-military buildings being used as holiday homes along the shoreline around Portkil, but their needs were more permanent.

Margaret had left to get married but recently her husband had died and she had come home to the bunker to help her sister and bring a second pension. Their mother had died some time ago, Connie being the principle carer. And throughout this time she had worked in shops, occasionally babysat and tried her hand at a host of other things to make ends meet. But both were in or approaching their seventies and needed somewhere that was warm, wind and watertight for their old age. They had no heating in their bedroom and no adequate natural light – just more pill box slits with make-do windows. There was DIY wiring throughout.

My challenge was what to do. Their home failed that famous Below Tolerable Standard on points beyond counting: they had no proper kitchen, no proper bathroom, no running hot water apart from their DIY electric shower and the geyser in the kitchen, the wiring was dangerous, and their home was neither wind nor water tight. On a practical level their home was not fit for human habitation. I asked if they had considered council housing but the options were few, the most palatable a flat in the rougher parts of Helensburgh, over twenty miles away. There was little or no council housing in Kilcreggan. The old Scottish Special Housing

Association stock in Rosneath five miles up the road was too far for them and was family housing. They shopped by taking the ferry to Gourock so a move further from the pier made absolutely no sense and they were part of the community on Shore Road, and Kilcreggan itself. In a more interventionist age their home would have been condemned and a move forced on them but I knew from talking to people working in other Care and Repair schemes that a move away from the familiar and an individual's routines could be hugely harmful to their mental and physical health.

But being true to the mantra – mould the rules to help people, don't bend people to fit the rules – was proving to be almost impossible. I feared that the cost of an upgrade could leave them penniless, with grant limits set too low. They did say they would save what little money they had but it was a pittance and well short of the 25% that householders were asked to contribute under the old grant system. At that point, I don't believe there were 90% grants for those in poverty in Dumbarton District; that was a luxury I was able to use in Edinburgh because of Housing Action Areas. In Dumbarton Council I would have to help make the case for a policy change and then apply for this enhanced grant with no guarantee of success. And even if the Council were generous, the sisters didn't even have the 10%. Across Scotland Care and Repair bodies formed a mutual aid group, pooling experience and ideas, supporting each other and lobbying for change. I learned there that the problems faced by the Bunker Sisters were repeated across all rural communities, and that each care and repair officer had the same challenge finding resources and had developed the same skill at flying by the seat of their pants.

There was something about the service that brought out the best in local architects and consultants. I found one willing to do the initial work at risk and to cap his fees if it were successful to help make it work. He worked with the sisters and drew up plans and put some costings together. They were so pleased and grateful to have us working on their behalf but still steadfastly refused to get excited. This wasn't the first time someone had tried to help them, so why should they get their hopes up?

Despite a modest design and specification, the repair and improvement costs were prohibitive. However when compared to the cost of constructing a new house on the site or in the Peninsula for affordable rent, it made sense to preserve their home and keep their independence. The main point was to seize the momentum created by the establishment of

Care and Repair and start moulding those rules and powers to help people in a practical way. We were encouraged by the senior grants officer at the Council because they too wanted it to use its powers creatively and solve some problems. Tenders were sought and although I almost lost my nerve as the figures came in, my Council champions were not fazed. There had been a history of such requests being rejected in the recent past by a local authority with concerns about its limited private sector grant budget and in some political quarters a jaundiced view of the private sector. But they were determined. A report recommending both a 90% grant policy and the raising of the ceiling on the capital cost was put to the Council. I was on tender hooks, chewing what was left of my nails, but it came through. It was one of the most wonderful moments of my life to be able to tell the two patient and unflappable sisters that their grant had been approved.

But what about the 10%? Their meagre savings were not enough and even if they had been, how would two pensioners on benefits afford to pay to make it a home? And what about temporary accommodation whilst they had the work done? I remember that for the most part the ladies themselves created their own solutions. A neighbour with a holiday cottage on the hillside above their home offered them her place at a peppercorn rent. There were charitable funds. There was a Council common good fund. Somehow we got there and in six months their old home was transformed. It was largely cloaked in timber kit, working around the original footprint with some demolition. A new pitched roof was placed on top. The gun emplacement window was made larger and double glazed.

The sisters were so pleased and grateful. And when the paint was dry they allowed themselves a moment of joy and relief. No more autumns with a bucket of pitch for the roof, no more winters frozen to the bone. I went round to see them some months after it was completed and they had moved back in. They wanted to show their gratitude but had nothing. Margaret presented me with a string cloth she had knitted herself and one that, judging by the many years of useful service it gave me, had something of their resilience and strength.

Portkil was at the left hand corner of the saggy triangular patch that I covered, with Ardlui, past the top of Loch Lomond, at the apex and Bowling at its right corner. It was Bowling that presented me with my most intractable and complicated housing problem. And my greatest failure, at least on the face of it.

One of the driving forces behind the service's creation was a remarkable woman called Judith Midgely, who was the Council's representative on the Care and Repair Advisory Committee. The vast majority of cases referred by the Council came from the grants department but she gifted one that challenged my preconceptions about housing and my role on a number of different levels. At least the gun emplacement was a building of sorts, with foundations, a garden and a title.

In a strange way this Bowling challenge was also a legacy of conflict, although perhaps the link is a bit tenuous. Across Britain the massive housing shortage after the Second World War prompted a rise in people choosing to live on canals and navigable rivers like the Thames. Decades later the waterways were still recourse for those that couldn't afford a bricks and mortar home, or didn't like the sedentary lifestyle.

The case of the Bowling Boatmen does share with the Bunker Sisters those central questions for Care and Repair and this sort of intervention: what is a home, how does society support personal freedom of choice, and how important is that connection to place and community? In legal terms it was not a housing issue: they were not living in houses. At the same time it was about what half a dozen men considered to be home. That home: Bowling, sits at the end of the Forth and Clyde Canal. It was barely rural but somehow cut off from the two towns only a few miles away on either side. In the early nineties the semi-derelict little harbour marking the canal's end, was a relic, open to the River Clyde, with one or two distressed hulks littering the mud and the quayside. Above it sat an enclosed basin and above that, beyond the lock, a widened section of the canal. The canal had been built over a couple of miles away in Clydebank, so there was no navigable connection with industrial Scotland inland.

The file revealed a concatenation of difficulties: small personal ones like disrepair, fuel poverty, physical and mental ill health, linked with bigger national challenges about the legal status of housing and the commercialisation of national assets. Those problems interlinked in a way that made it almost impossible to find any safe solution. British Waterways were on a mission, tasked by successive Conservative governments to turn a profit and under pressure to sweat their assets. In charge of all publically owned canals, they were raising mooring fees and commercialising various sites in pursuit of the bottom line. In the case of Bowling, they were turning the basin into a yachting marina and had a planning application to extend the local hotel, develop up-market housing and build sports facilities next to it.

Decades had passed since the War but there were still those who preferred to live on barges and boats rather than a house or a tenement. Some had been driven there by personal circumstances, others by poverty. Bowling was host to dozens of people living part or full time on boats in the Basin, perhaps as many as a hundred folk. They were charged a modest mooring fee, matched by a fairly modest level of service: one cinder car park and one public toilet. The changes had started with a brutal rise in basin mooring fees and evictions for those boats deemed unfit. There had been a local campaign to stop the canal quango but it had fizzled out and just prior to my arrival, most of it had been emptied, replaced by new customers able to afford the higher prices. I was told that six boatmen remained, although they had been forced to decamp to the stretch of canal above the basin and warned they couldn't stay.

I wrote to their boat names, care of the basin. A neat and articulate response came but it warned me that the numbers had dwindled to four permanent inhabitants. I had been warned that they were difficult, and that there were tensions between some of the boatmen so I arranged to meet in the neutral territory of the pub next to the lock. What I wasn't prepared for was their diversity. They were all people that had held responsible jobs or had careers: a ship's engineer on the Clyde puffers, a design engineer, a Church of Scotland minister and an electrician-builder, but all had minimal incomes, being dependent on pensions and benefits. Their boats were very varied: a converted World War Two launch, a small yacht, a converted lifeboat, and a small canal pleasure boat. The builder was a lot younger than the rest, still in his late fifties, he could look after himself he said, but he was concerned about the rest. The other three had very different but serious and debilitating medical conditions: alcoholism, diabetes, dementia and chronic rheumatoid arthritis to name but a few. What they had in common, in addition to their aquatic lifestyle, was an absolute refusal to compromise on where they lived. These boats were their homes.

Even in the relaxed atmosphere of the public bar, they were all more or less suspicious of people in suits and certainly pessimistic about my abilities to help. But they did share their problems. Their boats were leaking and difficult to move about in. None had adequate heating and were either freezing in winter or, if they had a stove, in danger of suffocation. They were scared that they would be evicted at any moment. There were no decent facilities for personal hygiene on land, having to use the public toilets to wash, and shave in cold water, and despite the fact that they were getting less mobile, no concessions to their increasing infirmity.

I contacted a movement in England for the preservation of the rights of canal dwellers and with their help was able to take the boatmen's grievances to a meeting with British Waterways. The men were still paying mooring fees so I asked about their security of tenure and the quality of facilities on site, but the hand I was playing was poor and all I had in reality was some residual concern on the part of the quango about their public image. I walked away with no more than some stay of execution; they would not be evicted from their current berths until the area was redeveloped. It seemed that the continued slow progress of the planning system offered the best short term hope.

Despite this seemingly pointless situation they were a determined and hardy bunch of men. The law was absolutely clear, without a solum, a foot print on solid land; there could be no title and any repair or improvement grant. Judith worked some magic in the Council and secured some funding for materials and a lock-up, whilst Care and Repair committed a day a week of its new handyman service to repair the boats, fit handrails and new stoves. The boatmen really wanted to do the work themselves but were enthusiastic all the same, joining in when and where they could, but I think in all our hearts we knew that we were just buying a little time.

The ship's engineer went first. He had started to develop signs of dementia before we started but I think the disruption of the repairs made him deteriorate rapidly to the point where I knew I had to contact social work and he was found a place in a local care home. The builder disappeared, rumour had it that he had reconciled with his wife. The Reverend followed but not for some time. He was a marvellous man, full of knowledge and life but he didn't look after himself and had diabetes. But what heart and determination. He lost one leg but was insistent that he would stay on his boat. After struggling for months he became very ill, and almost died, then quickly lost his other leg. I went to the infirmary and with his son's help got him to agree to be housed in a Dunbritton flat which was adapted for wheelchair use. Around the same time the last engineer, now struggling to get himself in and out of the tiny yacht also agreed to take up a tenancy with the Association. They were all gone and the place had lost its heart. But there was one last drama. While the Reverend was recuperating from his amputation, the automatic pump he used to keep the leaking hull afloat ran out of battery and his boat went down. He was heartbroken. He had a life time of papers, of his own and others' journalism, his books on religion and in particular a collection of works by Kierkegaard, his love. All had perished. But although he was very ill in hospital he got one message to me asking if somehow, someone would rescue his family bagpipes. He had come from the Outer Hebrides and the pipes had been played in the trenches of the First World War by his father and by him during the Second World War. Through contacts in Dunbritton we managed to get a diver willing to recover the pipes.

The experiences and stories from Dumbarton and Clyde Care and Repair were challenging at the time, and so rich, featuring the most amazing examples of human endeavour and resilience that I have come across in my twenty five years in housing. And in the creativity and respect displayed by those that worked in Care and Repair across the country. What happened to the old lady at the start of my tale with the open fire and the life threatening outdoor loo? She refused to change anything, so what did Care and Repair do? They built a heavy plywood box around the inside of the WC, protecting the seat so that even in the event of collapse she could still use it. But stepping back, I think these stories tell us something fundamental about the connection between people and the places they live, their identity and pride. It also stressed for me the importance of humanity in looking at people's problems and not always looking for the big solution. It taught me a lot about what one might consider a home, about respect for people's choices, turning circumstances to your advantage and the adaptability of the human spirit. There was also a lesson there for me in the power of stories. I doubt Care and Repair would have managed to find those complex solutions to people's problems without the power of the stories that lay behind them, stories that persuaded bureaucracies to be flexible, pushed rules to their limits and prompted generosity. The last time I visited the Reverend he had a motorised buggy outside his flat for striking fear into motorists around Dumbarton. In his hand he was clutching a crisp new copy of Kierkegaard's collected writings, a gift from his son at Christmas and was warming a glass of malt between his hands. These are amongst the most powerful memories I have of work and by far the most satisfying.

One of the best things I've done
in my life . . .

East Lothian Housing Association

Peter Hayman.
Photo from East Lothian HA

Being a committee member can be all consuming, can be demanding, can be an educational experience, can be quite scary and can be very satisfying. It can be all of these. It is the voluntary committee member that sets housing associations apart from other social housing providers. And not everyone gives up their job to concentrate on the housing association. **Peter Hayman** *has been a committee member of East Lothian Housing Association since it started, and he recounts the development of the association, the changes that have taken place and how the association has adapted to or overcome the challenges.*

East Lothian Housing Association was formally inaugurated at its first Annual General Meeting in the Town House, Haddington, on the 25th May, 1988. Planning for its creation had started just under a year prior to this. I was first approached in June 1987 by Malcolm Duncan who at that time was the Chief Executive of East Lothian District Council (ELDC). He knew that I was a member of Notting Hill Housing Trust, one of the first housing associations to be set up in England, and therefore had some idea of what a housing association was. Discussions had clearly been going on in the Council about the possibility and feasibility of setting up a housing association in East Lothian.

Later that June the Council called a meeting to which they invited representatives from all the Community Councils in East Lothian and also members of the public. I went along as a representative of Gifford Community Council on which I then sat. The aim of the meeting was to see if there was sufficient interest among the public to set up a steering committee to consider if there was a case for setting up a housing association, and if there was, to plan for its creation. A committee of eleven was elected from that meeting, representing a wide range of people from East Lothian as well as two district councillors and one Council official. But other people came to our meetings as observers and facilitators, for example, Robin Burley, then CEO of Edinvar Housing Association (the precursor of Castle Rock/Edinvar), Derek King, representing the Housing Corporation in Scotland, and two ELDC officials who did a lot of the original legwork (Bruce Walker, Depute Head of Housing), and Rob Tinlin from the Planning department.

The Steering Committee met five times before calling a public meeting in November 1987 to present its conclusions and recommendations. Our discussions had centred around two issues: (1) What type of association did we want to be, and (2) should we aim to be independent right from the go or set up as a sub-group within a larger association such as Edinvar (which had already started developing in East Lothian). In order to deal with the first issue we paid a number of visits to different types of associations, for example, Lister Housing Co-operative in Edinburgh, the Newtongrange Sub-committee of Castle Rock Housing Association, and most importantly, Loreburn Housing Association in Dumfries.

At the public meeting in Haddington on 26 November 1987 I presented the Steering Committee's recommendations to the public. Before I did this we had an inspirational presentation from Brian Gegan, then CEO of Loreburn Association, in which he told us how they had set up their association and how it was organised. We also presented a report which had been drawn up by the Council (mainly by Rob Tinlin) entitled *'The Case for a Housing Association'*. The main gist of our report was to propose the setting up of a fully independent housing association (the majority view on the Steering Committee) and one closely modelled on Loreburn. Both recommendations were warmly received by the meeting and the committee. The text of the resolution was as follows:

'To form a Housing Association with the objectives:
1. *To assist in sustaining and regenerating communities in East Lothian primarily through the provision of good quality housing.*
2. *To provide a range of housing within the community for people in housing need.*
3. *To work in co-operation with statutory agencies, locally based voluntary*

groups and individuals to promote solutions to housing problems, and to seek registration with the Housing Corporation.'

Thereafter the Steering Committee under the vigorous chairmanship of Margaret MacKay, one of the two ELC councillors, set about applying for registration with the Housing Corporation and organising the first AGM at which a proper management committee could be elected.

The Case for a Local Housing Association in East Lothian

My personal reasons for getting involved in setting up ELHA came out of the experience of a struggle a few years earlier to prevent Lothian Regional Council from closing three of the rural primary schools near where I live. LRC's argument was that the roll call of these schools had fallen below a viable level as a result of the remorseless depopulation of the Hillfoot area of East Lothian. The Hillfoot is the area on the north slopes of the Lammermuir hills which run along almost the entire southern boundary of the county and includes villages like Humbie, East Saltoun, Gifford, Garvald, and Stenton. My own house sits part way up the side of these hills and, for part of the nineteenth century was the school and the schoolmaster's house for the tiny community of Longnewton. Many of the smaller schools like my house had closed long ago but all the larger villages still had their local school which was a focal part of the community. But not only were the local schools threatened by depopulation but so also were the village shops, the pubs, and the post offices.

This process of depopulation had been going on since well back in the nineteenth century as people moved off the farms into the towns where the work now was. But in the 1980s a new factor was emerging which was putting additional pressure on the ability particularly of young people to stay in the countryside, namely, the impact of Right to Buy (RTB). The villages of East Lothian's Hillfoot (like Gifford) are pleasant places to live and are particularly attractive to Edinburgh commuters (*mea culpa!*) and retirees. The Council stock in these villages was rapidly being sold off. Between 1980 and 2000 almost half the council stock in these areas had been sold; in a few villages 100% had gone. The dual impact of the loss of social rented housing and the rising prices driven by Edinburgh commuters was forcing young people to move out to the larger towns in East Lothian and into Edinburgh. Hence the falling roll calls of the village schools. To quote from the Council Report presented to the November 1987 public meeting:

More important than the level of housing need [in the Hillfoot villages] is the sheer number of applicants given the limited stock available. So few vacancies are generated that even applicants in pressing housing need may have to wait much longer than in the larger settlements. As a result people have to move from the smaller communities in order to get decent housing in a reasonable time. Indeed so widespread and well known is this situation that many people apply only for areas in the District where they know their needs will be met and in this respect waiting lists underestimate the extent of the housing problems in rural areas.

All this had become very clear to me when I was sitting on Gifford Community Council.

The obvious solution was to build some social rented housing in the villages and target families with children as the potential tenants. But this was precisely what the then Conservative government had made impossible for councils to do through the size of the discounts available to sitting tenants. East Lothian District Council had started to tackle the problem by building a few new council houses in Humbie which had one of the schools targeted for closure by Lothian region. It had also acquired sites in all the other villages but was now unable to build on them. Here precisely was how a housing association could solve the problem because its houses would be free of the RTB. In addition housing associations had access to Housing Action Grant (HAG) which, when we started, was at the very generous rate of 90%. Moreover, housing associations, unlike councils, were about to have access to private finance from the banks and building societies.

There was one other reason for setting up ELHA which had occurred to some far-sighted people on the Council. It was becoming clear that the Conservative Government was determined to sell off the 70,000 houses of the Scottish Special Housing Association (SSHA) as part of its privatisation programme. But councils were forbidden from bidding for these houses. They could only be sold to existing housing associations or new ones specially created for taking them over. There were about 700 of these houses in East Lothian and no local association in a position to bid for them if and when they came on the market. Creating ELHA was crucial to ensure that there would be a local association available to bid for them and hence keep control of them in local hands in East Lothian. Fulfilling this aim was to absorb a lot of ELHA's energies in the mid 1990s.

Setting up Shop

Immediately after the first AGM the new Management Committee met and appointed Roy Fawcett (one of the members of the Steering Committee) chairman and myself vice-chairman. Roy held this office for the first ten years of the Association and I held mine for fifteen years. The Council had generously given us a £35,000 start-up grant to which the Housing Corporation added £9,974 as 'seed-corn' grant with further grants of £11,900 in 1990 and £11,800 in 1991. With this money we were able to appoint our first staff. It was clear to us that our immediate need was to have a Development Manager to spark off our development programme and we were fortunate to be able to recruit to this post Sheila Kerr who had been a development officer with Whiteinch & Scotstoun Housing Association in Glasgow. Sheila subsequently became our Director and stayed with us until 2006. We set up our first office in a small shop at 66 Market St, Haddington, right opposite where our very much larger main offices are now located.

Inevitably we made financial losses in the early years but had broken even and begun to make surpluses by 1992.

Our First Developments – the Rural Programme

Although the primary reason for setting up the Housing Association was to address the crisis in rural housing in East Lothian, we had never intended to restrict ourselves to this. Hence the broad phrasing of the first of our objectives. Indeed, the key requirement at the beginning was to build as much stock as possible so that we could reach a viable size (through receiving acquisition and development allowances) before our seed-grant monies ran out. The Council was aware of this and transferred to us a number of its recently completed developments. From the Council's point of view this had the advantage of preventing these houses from subsequently being sold off under RTB. So the first development we obtained (March 1990) was sixteen sheltered houses in Cockenzie; the Council had a similar development next to our site and we came to an arrangement with them to share a warden and community services. Very soon afterwards we completed the refurbishment of twelve derelict ex-Coal Board houses in Ormiston (Clarks Buildings). These were allocated to young, homeless, people. These had been taken over by the Council who transferred them to us at nil cost.

Our first rural units came to us in August 1991, again by stock transfer from the Council – ten newly completed houses and two workshops in East Saltoun, and ten houses and two workshops in Dirleton (1991). Thereafter we built houses in nearly all the rural villages in East Lothian: seven houses in Garvald (1991), twenty-six houses in Gifford (1992), sixteen houses and two workshops in Stenton (1992), three houses in East Linton (1993), and sixteen houses in Pencaitland 1995). In 1995 we completed what we call 'the Rural Series'. This was a series of developments across several villages using the same contractor and the same house types, and all completed within four months of each other: fourteen houses in Whitecraig, five houses in Innerwick, sixteen houses and one workshop in Athelstaneford, and six houses in Elphinstone. Once again East Lothian Council was very helpful in expediting this for us.

I am particularly fond of our development in Pencaitland. Our houses are located in a strip of land (allocated to us by the Council under a section 75 agreement) which is right in the middle of an up-market private development. The developer, needless to say was not too happy about this, and neither were some of the first private owners. You could hear (not always under the breath) the sentiment: 'we don't want any of those kind of people here'. Nowadays, when friends come to visit us and I tell them about the Housing Association I sometimes take them to Tyne Park, Pencaitland, and challenge them to identify the socially-rented houses among the private houses. Only if they know something about the issue can they actually do it – our houses have no garages! Otherwise they fit in very well and we have had no neighbour issues at all.

Care & Repair East Lothian

In 1993 Care & Repair East Lothian became part of ELHA. This service was set up in East Lothian in 1987 by the Council and the Scottish Office Development Department and was managed by Shelter (Scotland) for five years. Since 1993 East Lothian Housing Association has acted as managing agent with revenue funding secured on an annual basis from East Lothian Council. Its core service is to assist clients to carry out essential repairs and maintenance or adapt their home to make it suitable for changing needs. Over the years its range of services to the community has grown and developed, particularly when we added our small repairs service in 2003 (boosted by extra staff in 2007). This provides a high quality service centred on minor repairs and assistance, focusing on those needs relating to the health and safety of clients. In 1998 we set up the East Lothian Care & Repair Trust as a registered charity with the aim of providing grants (usually about £500) to help people who were unable to fund the full amounts required for their recommended adaptations.

By 1995 we had built houses in nearly every village in East Lothian. **No village school has closed since ELHA was set up**. I count this one of our greatest achievements and one which is particularly gratifying to me personally, since this was one of my most important motives for getting involved in the first place.

So by the time the greatest challenge in our history took place (the SSHA stock transfer in 1996) we had about 300 houses in management. We had also established a presence in the towns of East Lothian (Prestonpans, Musselburgh, Haddington, North Berwick, and Gullane). This was important if we were to present ourselves as a credible bidder for the SSHA stock which was located in the towns and not the villages. We had moved to larger offices at 19 Hardgate, Haddington, and also recruited two key members of what became our Senior Management Team. Tracey Kerr joined us in 1993, initially on secondment from SSHA before she became our Housing Manager. Tracey had been the housing management officer who had looked after the SSHA stock in East Lothian – very helpful to us when we subsequently came to bid for this stock. Paula Oliver joined us in 1994 as our Finance Manager. Both Tracey and Paula have stayed with us ever since, Tracey now as Director of Housing Services and Paula as Director of Finance. We were now ready for the bid for the 650 SSHA houses in East Lothian.

East Lothian Housing
Association development.
Photo from East Lothian HA

Work nearly completed at
more East Lothian
Housing Association.
Photo from East Lothian HA

The 1996 Stock Transfer

The stock transfer was a prolonged and traumatic experience for both the staff and the Management Committee. We had known all along that a stock transfer of the ex-SSHA houses in East Lothian was on the cards. When the SSHA was abolished in 1989 and its properties were absorbed into the newly established Scottish Homes the transfers began in earnest with the creation of Waverley Homes in the Borders from the ex-SSHA stock in that area. Our turn came in September 1993 when, along with other Registered Social Landlords (RSLs) we were invited to bid for its East Lothian stock. At this time the stock consisted of about 700 houses but RTB was rapidly eroding this figure and by time of the transfer in February 1996 it was down to 632.

We were acutely aware that the independent existence of ELHA was probably dependent upon our success in this bid. In September 1993 we had less than 200 houses in management but in order to properly service our stock and our development programme we had seven full-time equivalent staff (plus the two staff of Care & Repair). There are undoubted economies of scale in having larger housing associations. Currently, with our much larger stock (1,300), we estimate that we would need just one extra member of staff to manage an extra 300 houses. We were well aware that at our rate of development at that time it could take ten to fifteen years or more to reach the level of about 1,000 houses which could ensure our long term survival as an efficient and independent organisation. In addition we were conscious that the strong political backing which had given us such a good start would be severely compromised if we failed to pull off this bid. But above all we were driven by the impetus which had got us going in the first place – a fierce desire to solve East Lothian problems by East Lothian people and to keep as much control as we could in East Lothian hands. Politicians who try to use the mantra of efficiency by, for example threatening the independence of the admittedly rather small East Lothian Council, have discovered that this East Lothian sense of identity is to be meddled with at their peril.

Rather surprisingly Scottish Homes decided to divide East Lothian into two ballot areas for the stock transfer, the East covering Haddington, Macmerry, East Linton and Dunbar, and the West comprising Tranent, Prestonpans, Wallyford, Whitecraig and Musselburgh. In the East ELHA was in competition with the much larger and long-established Cairn Housing Association, and in the West with the newly formed Melville Housing Association (at the time engaged in the stock transfer of the over 2,000 ex-SSHA houses in Midlothian). So our competitors were either (or about to be) very much larger than we were. But it was to be for the Scottish Homes tenants to decide whether their homes should be transferred and to whom.

So we had to set out to persuade the tenants that a home with ELHA was the best option for them and to persuade Scottish Homes that we were a viable vehicle for taking on this transfer. Preparing the bid was a lot of work for the staff but where we were able to score over our competitors was in actually being on the spot. We, the staff and committee, divided up the tenants between ourselves and went knocking on the doors to introduce ourselves to them in person. I'm sure that our trump card was the sense of East Lothian identity I mentioned earlier, but also that many tenants regarded us as the next best option to East Lothian Council which is the landlord many of them would have really preferred. The low level of council rents in East Lothian was well known to all, and indeed has been a constant issue for us. It is even possible that some tenants thought that ELHA was really a part of the Council, though we did try hard to explain the difference!

By the Autumn of 1994, when the Scottish Homes consultation was concluded with the help of an independent tenants' advisor, it had become clear that ELHA was the tenants' preference. Accordingly we achieved what was called 'Preferred Landlord Status', which meant that Scottish Homes would negotiate exclusively with ELHA for the transfer of the stock. The final decision would be dependent upon the result of a full ballot of all the tenants. We had assumed that from now on all would be relatively plain sailing. But it was not to be. These negotiations stalled for almost a year as Scottish Homes demanded a price for the houses which we felt would both undermine our long-time viability and prevent us from fulfilling the promises we had made to the tenants about new kitchens, bathrooms, double glazing, and central heating for those who did not have it.

This was a very tense time for us, putting a lot of pressure in particular on our senior management team of Sheila, Paula and Tracey, but they coped extremely well. Eventually the decision did go to a ballot in early 1996 but still without us having reached agreement on the price. The ballot was an overwhelming success for us – of the 77% of tenants who voted 93% voted to transfer their houses to ELHA. A date for the transfer had been fixed for 28 February and we now assumed that all would go smoothly ahead. But again Scottish Homes demurred. They were clearly being driven (presumably by their government masters) to squeeze as much out of us as they possibly could without regard (so I thought) for our long-term viability and the interests of the tenants. Our bankers (RBS) were in a difficult situation. Obviously the more we borrowed from them the better for the Bank, but at the same time they had to be sure that we could repay the loan! This all came to a head on the evening before the transfer was due to take place – an evening which I will never forget. Sheila, Paula, Roy Fawcett and myself, met at the prestigious RBS HQ in St Andrews Square Edinburgh with representatives of Scottish Homes and RBS, in order to hammer out a final settlement. Tracey was in the office in Haddington waiting to print out letters to the Scottish Homes tenants, giving the required one month notice of the rents we would be charging.

After about two hours of negotiations we were unable to reach agreement. Scottish Homes were demanding a price which we were simply both unwilling and, we felt, unable to pay. So the four of us made an enormous gamble, given what was at stake – probably the whole future of ELHA, and decided to walk out of the negotiations. This was about 9.30 p.m. We headed off to an Italian restaurant to get something to eat and left the Scottish Homes representative to get on the phone and go up the hierarchy until he found someone who could make the decision for him. You can imagine how tense that meal was and the relief when he walked in and said that Scottish Homes had agreed to the price we were prepared to pay. Even so we probably paid more than we should have. Well, as Paula said to Sheila, she got up in the morning as the Director of a housing association with 300 houses and went to bed as the director of one three times bigger!

The next day was also a memorable occasion for me and illustrated well the two radically different halves to my life. I left a meeting of the Faculty of Divinity at Edinburgh University where I taught Hebrew and Jewish Studies, and walked down The Mound from New College to the RBS HQ in St Andrews Square and sat down to sign, along with others, a loan for £7.2 million and the conveyances for 632 houses. This bifurcation in my life was eventually to lead to me retiring early from Edinburgh University in 2005 in order to concentrate on being chairman of ELHA.

Re-organisation and New Offices

Trebling overnight meant a major re-organisation of the Association and this absorbed a lot of our staff's energy in the following years. We took on six new staff, mainly in the areas of housing management and maintenance and created a new management structure based on departments of Finance, Property, Housing Management, Development and Care & Repair. We now had a pressing need for new offices. So in 1997 we moved across the road from 19 Hardgate into our first purpose built set of offices in 24 Hardgate – part of a larger sixteen unit development. We still have those offices today; they house the now much bigger Care & Repair department.

Homes for Life Housing Partnership

HFLHP was set up as a partnership between ELC and ELHA in an extremely rushed series of negotiations in December 1998 in order to meet an insanely short government timetable to access New Partnership money. Both sides saw this as the only way to access new government money for affordable housing in East Lothian at a time when Gordon Brown was sticking to the tight government expenditure plans inherited from the Conservatives with its inevitable impact on the HAG programme. New Partnership was one of those typical government initiatives (so common in housing policy since the Second World War), dreamed up for immediate political impact with no thought about how it might be sustained in the long term. ELHA got involved for the following reasons:

- It was one way of meeting our first aim as an organisation, namely, to address housing need in East Lothian.
- It gave us an extra amount of HAG (£600,000) – eventually spent on our only just completed site at the Maltings, Haddington.
- The initial plan was for HFLHP to be only a development organisation with all the services provided by ELHA, thus enabling us to spread our management costs over a larger stock and hopefully enhance our own financial viability.

We were clear on what we expected from the Partnership. My impression is that the Council were never clear about what they wanted from it. This lack of clarity at the outset (partially due to the very restricted timetable to which we had to work) has dogged us all the way along the line. The result is that things have not worked out the way either party expected. HFLHP was originally intended to be just a development vehicle but ended up turning into a fledgling housing association. We did initially provide the financial services to HFLHP but this did not work out to be economic for us. From the Council's perspective HFLHP never achieved its unit targets (500 houses in five years – never realistic), and it stalled at the 300 units which it now has.

When the funding and RTB rules changed and the Council could can again build its own houses it naturally saw no need to continue pumping money into HFL and hence brought its development programme to an abrupt halt in summer 2006. On our side the original reasons for being involved with HFL similarly evaporated. After a Communities Scotland inspection in May 2007 recommended major changes in the governance structure of HFL both the Council and ELHA withdrew their representatives from the board and it is now primarily a tenant-led RSL. However, ELHA did eventually come to supply its tenancy allocations (via Homehunt) and its maintenance services via our maintenance company R3.

Change of Leadership

At the AGM in 1988, after ably leading the Association for the ten years since its foundation, Roy Fawcett decided to resign as chairman. I had been expected to take over from him but just at that point I was asked by the University to take on a new and demanding administrative role which would have left me without the time or energy to do the role of chairman justice. Fortunately, Robert McNeil, a long term member of the Management Committee, was prepared to take it on, while I continued as vice-chairman. He completed five years as chairman and then resigned in 2003 to concentrate on his role as an East Lothian councillor. By that time I had served out my term as Head of Department and vice-Dean of the Faculty of Divinity at Edinburgh University and was taking a year off to complete a book on which I had been working for almost twenty years. So I was now in a position to take on the position of chairman of ELHA and I served in that role for the next eight years, having taken early retirement from the University in 2005.

Between Right to Buy and Falling HAG Rates

We continued to pursue our development programme after 1996 but its focus changed. Prior to this we had concentrated on the rural areas but apart from a few small rural developments our efforts were now centred on much larger sites in the East Lothian towns and larger villages. Homes for Life Housing Partnership was now building in the remaining rural sites being made available by the Council, using capital which would not have been available to us. But now we found ourselves in a trap which lay in wait for all the housing associations which had taken part in the SSHA stock transfers, especially those formed exclusively from this stock - namely, attrition through the Right to Buy. Just after the stock transfer we had approximately 930 units; in 2005 we had 983, despite developing 213 new units for social rent and twenty-six units for Shared Ownership. Basically we were just marking time.

ELHA was sheltered from the full impact of this process of attrition because we had an ongoing development programme, but it was not until we embarked on major developments like Barbachlaw in Ormiston (thirty-nine houses completed in 2006) and Windygoul in Tranent (eventually 140 houses, 2007–2009) that we really began to significantly grow our stock.

The other major problem we were encountering was the fluctuating total amount of capital being assigned by the government to the development programmes of housing associations and, in particular, the remorseless decline in the rate of subsidy available per house. This meant that we had to raise more capital through private borrowing from banks and building societies with the inevitable impact on the rents we had to charge. Moreover, while in the early years our development programme made a significant contribution to our overall financial viability now we were beginning to have to cross-subsidise it from our rental income. Eventually this created a serious ethical dilemma for our Management Committee and staff.

Another problem which became especially acute from 2003 onwards was the small size of our development programme. Normally it was possible to sustain this programme with just a Development Manager but in the good years there was sufficient work for two development staff members. In 2003 we appointed a development officer to assist the development manager but when the capital programme shrunk (it could fluctuate between approximately one and three million pounds) we found ourselves cross-subsidising the development department. Then in late 2002 Communities Scotland (which had absorbed Scottish Homes in 2001) proposed to transfer its RSL development funding budget to local councils. This was allied to strong pressure to reduce the number of developing associations in order to reap projected economies of scale – a fine policy for urban Scotland but which did not make a lot of sense for the rural areas.

East Lothian Council bid to become one of the first councils to take over this development budget and, accordingly, in August 2003 invited bids from six RSLs to manage its proposed affordable housing plan of building 2750 houses in the next ten years. The deadline for this bid was very short and put our staff under immense pressure, particularly as it was very clear that on our own we did not have the capacity to manage such a large programme. The threat to our independent development programme was very clear. What was also clear was that the loss of this programme would have a very serious impact on the morale of our staff, and especially on the Management Committee with so many of us having got involved because we wanted to make a positive contribution to the housing crisis in East Lothian by building new affordable rented housing. We had to put in a bid but we made it clear that we would be happy to collaborate with whoever else the Council chose as its preferred developer/s.

Our bid, along with the others, then went into a black hole and did not re-emerge until June the following year – rather galling, given the short time they had given us to prepare it. In the event we, along with Castle Rock/Edinvar (now part of the huge English RSL Places for People) were chosen as the Council's primary development partners in East Lothian. Although this was a very welcome outcome for us it placed us in a dilemma: did it make any sense for us to attempt to compete for HAG funding with an organisation the size of Castle Rock/Edinvar (with PfP behind it)? So began a major reappraisal of our future which took up a lot of our time and energy in 2005–6.

The Options Appraisal and the Knowles Report (2005–6)

In the aftermath of the effort to achieve 'Preferred Developer' status with the Council and also our rising concerns about the long-term maintenance costs of our stock it became clear to us that we required a major reappraisal of where we were and where we should be going in the future. Accordingly we commissioned two consultants' reports, one from Dave Alexander on our options for the future and one from Knowles Consultancy Glasgow on our maintenance programme. The first stage of the Alexander options appraisal gathered the opinions of the staff and the committee on our present position and laid out the possible ways forward. He presented these options to our membership at our 2005 AGM:

- the status quo

- buy in services from another association
- became part of another group of housing associations, or
- transfer of engagements, i.e. merge with another association

From the subsequent discussion and questions it was clear that our membership shared the overwhelming feeling of our committee and staff that, if at all possible, we should aim for a result which preserved as much as possible of our independence.

So in early 2006 we invited six neighbouring and much larger RSLs to suggest how they would be prepared to solve our problem about development and what constitutional arrangements that might entail. It turned out that most of the responses would have meant some loss of ELHA's independence, usually by moving into a group structure. However, Castle Rock/Edinvar (CR/E), without putting in a formal bid, suggested that the way forward for us might be a development partnership which would involve, yes, the loss of our development department but would preserve our full constitutional independence.

So, at our June 2006 Management Committee meeting, we decided that the CR/E proposal was the best way of both maintaining our independence and delivering the HAG programme for the Council. It did involve basically sharing out the HAG budget for East Lothian with CR/E and transferring our one remaining development officer to Places for People (who delivered the development services for CR/E). So at the 2007 AGM I had the great pleasure of ritually signing the 'East Lothian Strategic Alliance' with Alistair Steele, the CEO of Castle Rock/Edinvar. As it turns out this arrangement has worked very well for both partners – co-operation has been very much better for us and our customers than competition. So now PfP provides all our development services but with significant input from our own staff and constant consultation with us. The Council also seems to be happy with this arrangement.

The eighty-five page Knowles Report comprehensively surveyed our current procedures for maintaining our stock and made a number of suggestions for how they might be improved. But the Report offered little hope for us to significantly cut what we perceived to be the unsustainable level of the prices we were paying for the reactive and planned maintenance of our stock. So the Report was disappointing and, in my view, quite possibly a waste of money. Perhaps this was a useful lesson to us that calling in consultants is not necessarily the best way to solve our problems. Nevertheless, this experience prepared the way for, and made us receptive to, the dramatically new direction that we would be taking from the Autumn of 2006 onwards.

Retaining the Excess Right to Buy Proceeds (2005–2011)

In the initial Sale and Purchase agreement for the stock transfer in 1996 an estimate was made of the likely Right to Buy receipts we would receive over the next ten years. Any surplus achieved over and above these estimated amounts was to be kept in an escrow account and returned to Communities Scotland in 2006. By 2006 there was about £800,000 in this account. As it turned out the initial agreement had wildly underestimated the level of RTB sales but also, we felt, had underestimated the long-term costs of maintaining and improving the stock. By fortunate co-incidence our finance staff had already by 2003 calculated that the Net Present Value (NPV) of the transfer stock was about £800,000 less than the price we had paid, i.e. that was about how much more we had paid than we should have done. We were not alone among transfer stock associations in feeling this way, and hence the battle lines were being drawn up for a major confrontation between the housing association movement, Communities Scotland and the Scottish government.

With the help of the Scottish Federation of Housing Associations and our MSP John Home Robertson we were able to get the concession from Communities Scotland that we would be able to keep the proceeds of all future RTB sales. But negotiations continued over the £800,000 since we wanted to ensure that any changes to the Sale and Purchase agreement would not invalidate the warranties and guarantees we obtained from Scottish Homes at the time of purchase. As it turned out we really needed those guarantees when asbestos was found in some of our transfer stock in Prestonpans. It took until 2011 before we were finally allowed to keep the £800,000. This was a very welcome addition to our bottom line, especially since in 2009 we had committed £647,000 to buying out our landscape maintenance contract with East Lothian Council. Henceforth we would not have to cover the cost of maintaining the landscape areas around our properties. The extra finance also made it easier for us to work towards achieving the Scottish Housing Quality Standard for all our houses. Otherwise we might have struggled to meet the 2015 deadline for this. This particular line of argument was quite influential for persuading Communities Scotland and the government to allow transfer RSLs to keep these RTB proceeds. Just for once they conceded that they could not impose new targets on us without giving us the finance necessary to achieve them.

New Directions

After having seen us through the complexity of the Options Appraisal process Sheila decided to make a complete change of career and handed in her resignation as Director in June 2006. I was delighted when Martin Pollhammer, then acting director of Corporate Services for Scottish Borders Housing Association (SBHA), applied for the post. Despite his relative youth in comparison with the other people on our shortlist he greatly impressed us with his energy and enthusiasm and exciting new ideas for how we could develop ELHA in the future. Prior to Scottish Borders Martin had been the Housing Manager of Berwickshire Housing Association and while there developed and marketed the online, choice-based Homehunt system of allocating tenancies which we had ourselves already adopted. Martin was appointed to the newly named post of Chief Executive and took office in October 2006.

There followed a Committee Awayday on 18 November 2006 at which we had a presentation from Duncan MacKay of SBHA on the new IT driven maintenance service which he had been pioneering, while Martin presented his ideas about moving to a new web-based system of delivering our tenant services. In this system as well as people being able to access all our core services (such as applying for houses, rent payment, repairs reporting, anti-social behaviour reporting and information and advice services) twenty-four hours a day, the website would include our 'On-Line Housing Office' – which we would open during office hours to deal with all enquiries on-line and in real time. This would be a real innovation in service provision in our sector. The Management Committee readily agreed to pursue all these new ideas but especially the possibility of bringing our repairs service in-house by setting up a new maintenance company subsidiary. This way we could save on the profit element incorporated in the contracts with our existing contractors and also on the VAT we had to pay. In addition, and most importantly, we should be able to offer a better, more responsive, service to our tenants.

On-line Housing Office, Launch of R3, Group Structure, New Offices

There followed a period of frenzied activity as we launched the new 'On-line Housing Service' in 2007, and recruited Duncan MacKay in 2009 as our Director of Asset Management to prepare for the launch in 2010 of our new maintenance subsidiary company which we decided to call R3 (Respond, Repair, Rebuild). To house a major expansion in the scope of our activities we urgently needed new offices and in 2009 acquired an iconic building in Market Street, Haddington, whose latest stage of a long previous life was as the offices of the East Lothian Courier. This was a major renovation project out of which, along with the new offices, we also managed to create fourteen new housing units. The whole staff were re-organised into a new group structure. We moved into our new renovated offices in March 2010 just in time for the launch of R3.

R3 uses a 'work scheduling system' which allows customers to book appointments, and sends text messages such as appointment reminders and the name and expected arrival time of the operative who will carry out the work. Our on-line service allows customers to report their repair twenty-four hours a day, and select their own appointment slot themselves. R3 now provides maintenance services, not just to ELHA, but to a range of housing associations and other private businesses and individuals across the Lothians, Edinburgh city, and the Scottish borders.

Development Troubles

While all these major changes were taking place we continued to develop at a fairly steady rate: thirty-nine units in Wallyford (2006), fifty-four in Tranent in 2007 (heated by ground-source pumps), twenty-four in Musselburgh (2008), forty-two in Tranent and five in Bolton (2009), sixty-nine in Prestonpans and twelve in Tranent (2010), forty-four in Tranent (2011), and then twelve in Haddington (2012). The development at Bolton Steading

and the subsequent developments were all funded by an innovative arrangement which we reached with East Lothian Council. They agreed to provide
us with a £25 million borrowing facility whereby they borrow at very
advantage rates from the Public Works Loan Board and then on-lend to us
with a very low mark-up to cover their costs. The interest rate achieved is
very much less than it would cost us to borrow on the commercial markets
from banks or building societies. However, this was not sufficient to save
our development programme from the catastrophic effect of the 'credit
crunch' in 2008 and its consequent effects on the amount of HAG available
and the drastic cuts in the grant available per house. When the grant fell to
£40,000 per house we were unable to continue developing without serious
damage to our overall finances or significant rises in our rents.

How were we to react to this? Like many other developing associations
we began to look at alternative tenures (mainly what is called 'mid-market
renting') which required far less state grant aid but addressed a clientele
which could afford to pay more than the social housing rents we charged
but could not afford to buy on the open market. In 2011 we spent
considerable time discussing a proposal to go into partnership with a
developer who was able to access funding via private equity sources for a
major programme of mid-market renting. In the end we decided not to
go down this route, not only because it would have been a departure from
what the Management Committee regarded as our primary purpose, but
also because the proposed arrangement seemed to leave all the profit with
our private sector partners and all the financial risks with us.

Some other Scottish RSLs, mainly the bigger ones or those which were
part of much larger UK wide associations, continued to develop at these
low subsidy rates. The larger an association was the better the borrowing
rates it could get in the market and the easier it was to draw on reserves or
cross-subsidise development from its other sources of revenue. Then we
began to see a worrying (to me at any rate) trend of smaller associations
being swallowed up by larger ones and especially a serious drop in the
number of developing Scottish RSLs. No doubt some economies of scale
could be achieved this way, but at what cost to the independence and local
base of our housing movement? ELHA decided not to go down this route
and we called a halt to our development programme. Our main concern
was an ethical one: if we were to continue to develop it would mean
putting up our rents far beyond the inflation plus 1% which was our

Shared Ownership – ELHA's Experience

The second development which we completed (April 1990) was four shared ownership houses in Haddington. Thereafter until 1997 many of our developments contained an element of shared ownership (SO). Since shared owners purchased part of their houses (usually at the start 25%) these required less HAG from Scottish Homes. This meant that, with the HAG averaged across the whole development (social-rented plus SO), we could develop our social-rented houses at a slightly lower HAG rate and so charge lower rents. We would also be helping out a range of people to get onto the housing ladder who might otherwise have been cut out of private ownership but too well-off to easily get social-rented housing.

But as time went on it became clear to us that this form of housing tenure has serious difficulties and eventually we decided to do no more of it. The main problem with SO is that, although the owner/tenant may own only 25% of the house they are responsible for 100% of its maintenance. The rent they pay for the 75% of the house which they don't own is slightly reduced to compensate for this but they still end up paying rent plus a mortgage, and extra legal fees every time they want to 'staircase-up' and buy another tranche of the house.

Originally it had been hoped that owner/tenants would mostly staircase-up by 25% tranches as their incomes grew and hence come to own the whole house. But, as things turned out, hardly any of them have done this. Many of them have struggled with maintenance costs as the houses have got older. A few of our SO houses have even been subject to statutory repairs notices.

For these reasons the Management Committee decided not to continue with SO but to concentrate on the social-rented housing which we regarded as the primary purpose for which the Association was set up. In some respects a better way of subsidising rural home ownership is the arrangement we administer, on behalf of the Council, for ten houses each in Ormiston and East Saltoun. ELC provided the land, Scottish Homes provided Gro-grant to the builder and the properties were sold outright to people with low incomes and a connection to the rural parish for around 57% of the open market value. Legal agreements ensure that if the properties are sold they are sold on to qualifying purchasers for 57% of current market values or the subsidy is repaid.

We had to return to this issue of alternative tenures many years later when we gave serious consideration to getting involved in mid-market renting.

regular yearly increase. Why should our tenants who came from the less well-off strata of society bear the burden of housing those in desperate need of accommodation? Surely this was a burden that should be carried by the whole of society, and especially by those who were better off and comfortably housed themselves.

We built no houses in 2013 and 2014 but devoted our energies to supporting the campaign of SFHA to persuade the Scottish government to put the HAG subsidy rates back to a level which would allow us to restart developing. In the end the campaign succeeded, very definitely helped by the fact that with a devolved Scottish government we could actually get to and persuade the people who make the decisions. The English RSLs have fared far worse than the Scottish in this respect and their HAG rates (where grant is available at all) are dismally low. We have now begun to build again and should complete seventeen houses in 2015 and thirty-five in 2016. We reckon we can develop at this rate for the foreseeable future but it goes nowhere near what is needed to meet the desperate housing need in an East Lothian so close to the very resilient Edinburgh housing market which puts such pressure on local house prices and the cost of development land.

The Bedroom Tax

The bedroom tax, or to give it its proper name 'the under-occupancy charge', was from April 2013 a problem we could have done without. Like other RSLs and councils we were already experiencing a growth in rent arrears as a result of the recession following the 2008 'credit crunch'. We felt acutely the unfairness of this charge and also the fact that it conflicted in some cases with our own allocation policies. Here we were able to play a significant part in at least mitigating its effect in Scotland. We developed a policy which allowed us to write off tenant arrears in cases that conflicted with our own policies or would, in our opinion, have driven our worst-off tenants into dire poverty. We contacted Iain Gray our MSP and he raised our policy in the Scottish Parliament. It was then accepted as a viable way of mitigating the impact of this charge. Fortunately, as the result of new powers to be granted after the Referendum, it now looks as though the Scottish Parliament should be able to formally abolish the charge in Scotland.

Conclusion

The major thread which runs through almost the whole of this history of ELHA is our determination to remain true to our roots as a locally based and locally run organisation. We have benefitted enormously from the steadfast support we have received from the wider community and especially from East Lothian council and all the political parties who have run it whether Labour, SNP/Lib Dem or now Labour/Conservative. We have an excellent staff and a Management Committee many of whom have been with us for a very long time, two of us since the Association was founded twenty-seven years ago. Plans for the future include a significant development of our on-line services and spreading more widely the customer base of R3 into the private market.

All three of the aims we set out when we founded East Lothian Housing Association have been achieved. We are by far the largest RSL in the county with about 1,300 houses under management. We have made a significant contribution to solving the housing shortage in our area, in particular in the rural areas which were my initial major concern. The quality of the service we provide to our customers has been widely recognised. We were a finalist in the 'Small Social Landlord of the Year' category in the 2013 UK Housing Awards in London and shortlisted in the same category in 2014. We were a finalist at the Housing Excellence Awards in 2013 in Manchester and won the 'Innovation of the Year' category at the 24 Housing Awards in 2013 in Birmingham. Our staff achieved the Healthy Working Lives Gold Award in 2013 and our R3 maintenance company has a won a whole string of awards for innovation and the quality of its services.

Obviously we have not solved the severe housing shortage problems in East Lothian. That would require a much larger input of public capital than any of the political parties are willing to provide, and a radical approach to the numerous blocks on the release of land for development. But we can pride ourselves on the fact that the situation would have been very much worse if we had not existed. For me personally, being involved in ELHA has been one of the best things I have done with my life.

A Border Ballad

A regional case study

Peter Lee.
Photo Peter Lee

*The Scottish Borders have always had a unique approach to life. Housing is no different. **Peter Lee** who was the Director of Eildon Housing Association for nearly thirty years tells the story of how housing associations developed in the Scottish Borders and became the only providers of social housing in the region. The regional case study is drawn around the Eildon story from its small beginnings connected to the local psychiatric hospital to being a Regional Association providing support to other associations and Peter's key role within it.*

My introduction to the world of housing associations began in 1983 when I joined the Scottish Federation of Housing Associations as its Research and Policy Officer. This appointment was one of the best introductions anyone could have to the housing association movement in Scotland. The Housing Corporation in Scotland (HCiS) and the SFHA worked closely together to influence the Scottish Office to increase investment to Housing Associations which proved largely successful. As the HAG programme became an increasingly significant part of investment for social housing in Scotland it was inevitable that questions would be raised particularly in the rural parts of Scotland as to how resources were allocated with the vast majority of funding quite understandably going to urban Scotland.

In 1984 the SFHA formed a working party to look at rural housing provision, inviting those housing associations with an interest to contribute. I was the facilitator of the working party responsible for setting the agenda, providing statistical data and writing the minutes. A member of the group was a certain Mr Jimmy Millar representing Eildon Housing Association. Jimmy said very little and was clearly there to observe. Little did I know then that I was to see a lot more of Jimmy in his role as Honorary Secretary of Eildon and someone who seemed to know everyone of importance in the Borders, which was to prove very beneficial when I joined Eildon the following year.

The problem facing the SFHA was to support the concept of housing associations working in rural areas without jeopardising the success of the Area Renewal and Special Needs programmes which were the lifeblood of most the established SFHA Members. The SFHA could not therefore be seen to be supporting rural housing if it resulted in a reduction of funds for Area Renewal and Special Needs.

Some of the largest housing associations in Scotland provided Sheltered Housing schemes for the Elderly across Scotland including many located in small rural towns. They understandably wanted to carry on developing in any part of Scotland where a need was identified. It was becoming increasingly clear however that HCiS wanted to address the inequalities in the funding regime as it affected the needs of rural areas and were beginning to explore ways of addressing the issue. One way forward was to create all-purpose regional housing associations located in rural parts of Scotland which were inadequately served by the existing network of housing associations across Scotland.

As a result, informal discussions started to take place with existing housing associations who were located in these areas to see how likely they were to be able to expand to play a more strategic role. Unbeknown to me, Eildon were already having discussions with HCiS as a possible candidate for channeling housing association investment to the 1800 square miles of the Scottish Borders.

So it was that in March 1985 a rather insignificant advert appeared in The Scotsman. Eildon Housing Association was seeking a Director. I became curious and made informal enquiries with my contacts in the Scottish Office and HCiS. Although no formal agreement had been made, it was clear that HCiS was willing to channel the HAG programme for the Borders through Eildon if it agreed to appoint staff and open an office. It now became clear why Jimmy Millar had attended the Rural Working Party meetings and why he had said so little. As I was to learn later, Jimmy was a shrewd operator, quite capable of acting the daft laddie when it suited his cause. Eildon were not then members of the SFHA and Jimmy used the meetings in the SFHA offices to gauge the support or opposition to the idea of Regional Housing Associations.

As soon as I saw the advert I thought I should find out more about

Eildon. The idea of starting a new housing association almost from scratch appealed to me. After all, an opportunity like this did not happen very often. I duly phoned up Jimmy Millar to say I was passing through Melrose the following Saturday and could I call in for a chat. I was told to arrive at Burt's Hotel in Melrose at 10.30 to meet a few Committee Members, which I duly did. When I arrived I met about half the Committee including the Chairman Bill Wilkie. They all seemed genuinely impressed that I had taken the bother to come down to meet them and they soon started to quiz me about how I saw things developing and the level of funding they might expect to get. We all seemed to get on very well and following a formal interview process a few weeks later, I was offered the job and started work that summer.

On my way back to Edinburgh, following my first day in the job, it began to dawn on me what I had done: I was now the proud owner of Jimmy Millar's filing cabinet which contained all the official documents of the Association, an old desk and chair and an IBM typewriter with a distorted letter 'O'. My office was a single room in the offices of our Treasurer, next to the Ship Inn in Melrose. When I explained to Jimmy that I could not type he immediately offered the services of his daughter in law who would collect anything for typing on her way to nursery school and return the finished products in the afternoon on her way to pick up her children. It was difficult to envisage in those early days how successful we were to become. What I quickly learnt was how committed and knowledgeable the Committee were and how easy it was to meet those key people in the Borders who made the decisions and how helpful they all were.

Most importantly of all was my luck in having Bill Wilkie as Chairman, who shared the same vision as me; wanting to create effective Regional Housing Association serving the Borders. Bill was well respected throughout the Borders and was an excellent chair of meetings and a great ambassador for the association when negotiating with politicians, officials, consultants and the like.

Bill gives his own account of the early days: *'I first got involved with Eildon Housing Association in 1978 when had just three properties which had been purchased and upgraded to provide care in the community (known in those days as half way houses) for people who otherwise would have to be cared for in Dingleton Psychiatric Hospital. Upgrading the properties proved to be more expensive than had been envisaged and as a result the Association was in*

Bill Wilkie.
Photo from Eildon HA

financial difficulty. Thankfully this was overcome by Ettrick and Lauderdale District Council giving a Grant to the Association to solve the immediate crisis

It soon became clear to me that Eildon would only become viable if it increased its estate and generated sufficient revenue income to allow it to employ professional staff. All the input up to this point had been made on a voluntary basis.

The first task was to strengthen the Committee structure and bring new Members on board who had a detailed knowledge of their local area and who were passionate about providing good quality housing for those in need.

The next step was to convince The Housing Corporation of our aspirations and that we were competent to execute a viable programme. I am happy to say they were sympathetic to our proposals and agreed to fund a programme that allowed us to build around a hundred houses a year. The rest as they say is "history" and despite the many changes in funding, procurement, legislation etc., I am pleased to say Eildon has continued to develop and increase its provision of affordable housing for those in need throughout the Borders'.

Housing in the Scottish Borders

Before Local Authority reorganisation, the Borders had five local authorities for a population of just 105,000. Most people live in the thirty or so small towns and villages, from the high hills of Tweeddale to the west to the rolling farmland of Berwickshire and its coastline to the east. Few settlements are far from the River Tweed and its tributaries with Peebles, Galashiels, Selkirk, Hawick and Kelso the main towns.

Although close to Edinburgh and the Lothians, the Scottish Borders jealously guards its own identity and traditions. This was to benefit Eildon who were seen as a wholly Borders based organisation whose sole interest was to bring housing investment to the Borders, Having this clear geographical identity greatly assisted me in quickly getting the support of the local authorities who each saw our new role as a positive move and therefore willing to cooperate in identifying potential sites and identifying priority need.

The target set by the Committee following their discussions with HCiS was a hundred house completions a year. This would enable us to grow to a 1,000 houses in ten years which was regarded as the size we needed to be to be financially stable. At the outset I was encouraged by the Committee's desire to build quality developments which blended in with the local environment. There was to be no standardisation which had resulted in so much of the social housing in Scotland, including the Borders, being so uniform and dreary. Our developments were to be well designed homes located in existing communities close to local amenities. Mixed developments were to be encouraged wherever there was a need with special needs housing being integrated into general needs developments. Architects were encouraged to bring forward developments capable of winning national housing awards, Our Committee took a keen interest in the proposals presented by our design teams and it wasn't long before we started to win Saltire and Civic Trust Awards.

With so much development activity, Eildon set up a Development Sub Committee to oversee the rolling development programme. To create a hundred completions a year with developments located in each of the four Districts, ranging in size from half a dozen houses in the smaller villages to thirty unit developments in the towns, required us to acquire around half a dozen sites and to be working up designs on another half dozen, with a further half dozen on site. At any one time, there could be up to twenty different developments progressing from inception to completion.

This rapid change of pace was my first priority. The members of the Development Sub Committee expected to be fully involved in approving each site prior to acquisition and the design proposals submitted by the Design Teams we appointed. They also wanted to see the developments being built and soon became very adept at asking the right questions.

Some of my happiest memories of those early years were the site visits we planned for our Committee Members. These were all day affairs held every couple of months. Meeting in the office for a quick briefing, each Member would be given a set of papers which contained site plans of those sites we wanted to acquire along with plans and elevations of those schemes on site. We would then pile into a couple of cars and start our journey, often covering over a hundred miles and visiting half a dozen sites. As important as these visits were to ensure our development targets were being met, they had another very important function. With such a dramatic change in the scale of our operation, there was a need to gain quickly the confidence of the Committee in order to obtain the delegated authority required to run an efficient organisation. These site visits enabled us all to get to know each other better and build up the trust required to run an effective voluntary organisation. An important aspect of a successful day visiting sites was the choice of the local hostelry selected for lunch. Fortunately the Borders is well endowed with hotels and pubs that provide a good lunch and my knowledge of the Borders and some of the local characters was greatly enhanced over a relaxing lunch.

Much to my surprise, my first year with Eildon flew by and we were on our way. Our development programme was going well and we were accepted as the recognised social housing developer for the Borders. Over the next twenty-five years we continued to provide a rolling programme of housing developments across the Borders Region. As our reputation for delivering a successful and varied development programme grew, we started to be approached by other rural housing associations for assistance with their own development programmes. From my days of working at

Old Town, Peebles.
Photo from Eildon HA

the SFHA I had always been impressed in the way housing associations shared information. Most rural housing associations became members of RIHAF, the Rural and Islands Housing Association Forum, which was set up by the SFHA as a mechanism for rural housing associations to meet and discuss common problems.

Eildon was a founder Member of the Forum and played an active part in supporting its aims and objectives. We soon found ourselves with one of the largest development programmes in rural Scotland and were responsible for delivering the development programmes of Carrick Housing Association and Rural Stirling Housing Association.

By 1990, just five years after Eildon began its new role as a Regional Housing Association within the new framework with Scottish Homes, there could be no doubt that this experiment to increase development opportunities in rural areas using a local housing association was a successful model, fully vindicating the HCiS confidence in promoting this model.

Integrating housing and care services

The Scottish Borders has always had a reputation for developing new ideas for helping people with learning disabilities and the frail elderly, including those with dementia. Much of the pioneering work for what we now call 'Care in the Community' was developed by a small team of psychiatrists and social workers under the charismatic leadership of Doctor Dan Jones at Dingleton Psychiatric Hospital in Melrose. One of the results of this work was the creation of a charitable housing association who with the help of Ettrick and Lauderdale District Council acquired a few houses in Melrose, Selkirk, and Galashiels which were used as accommodation for people with learning disabilities with appropriate support provided in the community by Health Board and Social Work staff.

This was how in 1973 Eildon Housing Association was formed, and why it has always played such a positive role in the development of innovative care provision. Eildon's Committee has always supported the concept of integrating housing and care services. Two of the key Members responsible for guiding the Committee through this often controversial area were Margaret Auld, a former Chief Nursing Officer for Scotland, and

Donald MacDonald, a former Director of Social Work at Borders Regional Council.

Both Margaret and Donald were keen supporters of Care in the Community initiatives and both played a vital role in supporting staff in the development of new types of provision and services. Donald Macdonald explains: '*Eildon Housing Association started in the early 1970s, from a need to provide suitable accommodation in the community for patients discharged from Dingleton Psychiatric Hospital in Melrose. Local authority housing in those days was largely concerned with the provision of housing for families. The concept of Sheltered Housing was not then well established in Scotland by Local Authorities and the elderly were placed in Residential Homes run by Welfare Departments. Many of these "Homes" were either former "Poor House Accommodation" or adapted large houses. Facilities were often basic with many residents having to share bedrooms.*

In Scotland, the separate Health, Welfare and Children's Departments were brought together in 1969 through the Social Work [Scotland] Act that created Social Work Departments. A number of Directors of Social Work in Scotland were appointed who had served in senior posts in Children and Welfare Departments in England and Wales. They were familiar with a wider range of Community Care Services and often found people in residential homes would rather be recipients of community care in their own homes.

In the Borders, Dingleton Psychiatric Hospital was one of the most progressive psychiatric hospitals in Scotland with a philosophy of wanting to care for more of their patients in the community rather than in the ward of a hospital. Unfortunately finding suitable accommodation in the community was difficult as the concept of providing housing for people with special needs was not a priority for local authority housing departments who were fully stretched trying to house the families on their waiting lists.

Eildon Housing Association made a very modest start to address this problem. Jimmy Millar the Secretary at Dingleton Hospital and a few senior Psychiatric Nurses and Social Workers formed a Charitable Housing Association as a means of providing a few houses in the surrounding area. Russell Sanderson [now Lord Sanderson] a local business man was approached to become their Chairman and they were successful in obtaining a grant from the Scottish Office to buy their first house above a shop in Melrose High Street.

In 1982, Bill Wilkie was appointed Chairman and under his leadership began to expand. As Estates Manager for Borders Health Board and a part time lecturer in Building Construction at Edinburgh University, Bill had the experience needed to guide the Association to expand into an effective provider for the whole of the Borders.

When Peter Lee was appointed in 1985 as Eldon's first member of staff, Eildon were fully supported by The Housing Corporation and had an ambitious development programme in the pipeline. It was clear to me that as Director of Social Work that we needed to work closely together to create better opportunities for those people with special housing needs.

When I retired a few years later I was invited to join Eldon's Committee of Management and was impressed by the role Eildon was able to play in the provision of Community Care. We developed a number of innovative developments for a wide range of needs including Sheltered and Extra Care Housing for Older People, A Care Home for People with Dementia, and Supported Housing for People with Learning Disabilities.

It is most gratifying to how Eildon has grown from its humble beginnings into one of Scotland's most effective and respected Housing Associations'.

Millar House Melrose.
Photo from Eildon HA

The following examples give a flavour of the variety of care and support services that Eildon has developed over the past thirty years.

Helping Abbeyfield Societies to improve their facilities for the frail elderly

During the early 1990s, a number of Abbeyfield Societies in the Borders were finding it difficult to provide the expertise and resources necessary to improve the accommodation and services needed for the increasingly frail group of people in their residential homes.

Most Abbeyfield Societies in the Borders owned a single large house with between six to eight residents, each with their own bedrooms and sharing a lounge and dining room. Meals would be provided by a housekeeper who would cook the meals and generally look after the place. Residents seldom had en suite bathrooms and there was little privacy other than their own bedrooms. Many of the buildings were in need of maintenance and required considerable capital investment to bring them to an acceptable standard.

A number of our Committee Members were also Committee Members of Abbeyfield Societies and it was therefore inevitable that Eildon would be approached to advise them on what could be done to improve their facilities. Constitutionally, individual Abbeyfields are charities and regulated by the Housing Regulator. The best way we could help them therefore was to absorb them into our own organisation through a process of Transfer of Engagements, We then applied for Housing Association Grant to improve the properties as part of our normal development programme

In this way Eildon acquired and modernised three Abbeyfield properties in Melrose, Jedburgh and Peebles.

Sheltered and Extra Care Housing for the Elderly

A number of Sheltered Housing developments had been successfully built and managed in the Borders by housing associations based in Edinburgh like Bield, Hanover and Kirk Care Housing Associations prior to Eildon being awarded development funding from The Housing Corporation. These developments were very popular and there was a need to build more. Eildon decided to include a number of Sheltered Housing schemes in the larger towns where a growing demand was identified. Despite some initial hostility to this from the well-established Sheltered Housing experts who thought they should be allowed to continue to build in the Borders, we successfully developed new Sheltered Housing developments in Peebles, Galashiels and Hawick.

As successful and popular as the standard thirty unit Sheltered Housing developments were we worked with our Social Work colleagues to develop the model further. In Peebles we built a communal dining room and kitchen, to enable tenants and other elderly people to join a lunch club guaranteeing them a good wholesome meal each day. In Galashiels we converted a residential home for the elderly and day care centre previously owned by the local authority into a modern Sheltered Housing Development with a kitchen, dining room and refurbished Day Centre available to the wider Community.

One of the most complicated joint ventures between Eildon and Scottish Borders Council was the replacement of a Residential Home for the Elderly at Dunwhinny Lodge in Peebles with a new Extra Care sheltered Housing scheme on a Council owned site on the other side of the town. From the beginning of the discussions to completion it was to take ten years and countless meetings with officials, residents and their families. Dunwhinny Lodge was a popular residential home, but it provided only basic bedsit accommodation for its twenty-four residents. It was beginning to show its age and despite its attractive setting was no longer fit for purpose. Eildon was approached to see how the accommodation could be improved. It soon became clear that converting the existing building into a sheltered housing type of provision would be impossible, even if alternative accommodation could be found for the existing residents. Relatives objected to the disruption this would cause for this frail group of people, who would be subjected to a double move. The only solution would be for Eildon to build the new replacement on an alternative site, move the residents into the new accommodation and then demolish Dunwhinny Lodge. It was agreed this was the preferred option and the hunt was on to find a site in the centre of Peebles. Following lengthy discussions with the Council, a site was identified which was used by the Roads Department as a Depot. They had a plan to relocate onto the outskirts of town and there was the possibility this would become available for our new development.

Architects were appointed to draw up proposals for the new development which was to be a state of the art Sheltered Housing Development, incorporating a number of novel features. Numerous meetings took place between Social Work, Health Board and Communities Scotland to agree the brief and how the development would be funded. Everyone was agreed that that the new development should be based on a housing model designed in such a way that allowed elderly tenants to receive whatever packages of care were needed without them having to move into a nursing home. Provision would be made to allow electric buggies to be parked outside a tenant's flat and additional bedrooms would be provided to allow carers or relatives to stay overnight to provide support when required. A range of other communal facilities was also included, like rooms for hobbies, hairdressing and a kitchen and dining facilities. Eildon would own the building and provide the normal housing management and maintenance services with Borders Regional Council's Social Work staff providing the support and care services. Each tenant would be individually assessed for their care and support needs and these were to be provided by Social Work and Health Board staff who visit the scheme when required.

This development at Dovecot Court was finally opened in June 2013 by Margaret Burgess MSP, Minister for Housing and Welfare. This development demonstrates what can be done if a multi-agency approach is adopted for the provision of housing and care for the growing number of older people requiring homes which are flexible enough to allow a wide range of services to be provided in a cost effective manner. In the economic climate following the financial crash, the need for different agencies to work collaboratively together will increase and this important development shows how this can be done.

Care Housing for People with Learning Disabilities

From its very inception, Eildon has always had an interest in providing care and support services for people with Learning Disabilities. As well as providing tenancies in our general needs stock with individual support packages provided by Social Work staff or specialist providers, Eildon has designed specific housing developments for this client group to provide a Supported Living Service for adults with Learning Disabilities. Our development at Station Avenue in Duns has provided a service for ten adults for over twenty years and over that time the service has continually changed, as good practice for this client group evolved with a growing emphasis placed on developing individuals' capacity for participation and independence.

Care Housing for People with Dementia

In 1995 discussions began between Eildon and Borders Health Board to explore the possibility of Eildon being able to help with the closure of Dingleton Psychiatric Hospital to meet the Government's aim to phase out long stay psychiatric hospital provision throughout Scotland. It was widely recognised that many of the long term patients in these hospitals were trapped in an entirely inappropriate environment because no alternative accommodation was available.

One such group were occupying a twenty-four bed ward at Dingleton, who, despite the best efforts of the dedicated nursing staff to make the environment more homely, could not provide them with the privacy and dignity they deserved. These individuals were mostly elderly people with Dementia.

It was not clear to me at first what we as a housing association could do to help. Housing Association Grant was given to housing associations to provide housing, not nursing homes. The first task for Eildon was to understand the capability of this client group and to this end I spent a couple of days shadowing Dawn McCraw, the head of the team caring for these people. What became self-evident almost immediately was how inappropriate it was that these people were in hospital. Equally self-evident was the desire of the nurses and assistants looking after these people to improve their quality of life which they were convinced would be achieved by providing a more domestic environment.

The real issue for us and Scottish Homes was whether this group of people would benefit from a residential home environment rather than a nursing home. We decided we needed some specialist advice and approached Professor Mary Marshall, a recognised expert in Dementia care from Stirling University.

Mary worked with us to help identify particular design issues specific to this client group. She also increased our confidence that people with dementia could benefit from a specially designed building and did not require the facilities found in a nursing home.

We appointed consultants to look at theoretical designs and, together with the expert knowledge of Dawn McCraw and Mary Marshall, agreed on a design of three linked houses of eight people per house, incorporating a number of unique design features to assist people with dementia to move

Bolton Steading in Haddington for East Lothian
Housing Association.

Photo: East Lothian Housing Association

The image of the rural housing association in 2015 –
Lochalsh and Skye Housing Association's Handyman service
– Donnie Morrison and Ruaridh MacKinnon.

Photo: Cailean Maclean for Lochalsh and Skye Housing Association

Cuddieside, Peebles – a rural town centre regeneration by Eildon Housing Association.

Photo: Eildon Housing Association

The innovative Craw Wood development for people with dementia by
Eildon Housing Association.

Photo: Eildon Housing Association

The entire community of North Ronaldsay turns out for an open day to celebrate the completion of the two family houses by Orkney Housing Association which provided a life line to the local community.

Photo: Orkney Housing Association

Award winning Grödians housing development in Lerwick for Hjaltland Housing Association. Incorporates high energy performance housing with flexible open-plan living areas and vibrant colour scheme. Street & building orientation is based around the Home Zone concept. Richard Gibson Architects.

Photo: Hjaltland Housing Association

Another award winning housing development and the first UK social housing scheme to be accredited by the German 'Passivhaus' Institute. Tigh-na-Cladach (house by the Shore) at Dunoon for Fyne Homes. Architect Gokay Deveci.

Photo: Fyne Homes

Happy family in Springbank Road in Doune. Rural Stirling Housing Association's development.

Photo: Rural Stirling Housing Association

around the building without getting disorientated. We were lucky in already having a site which ideally suited for this development and, following complex discussions between Scottish Homes, Borders Health Board and Scottish Borders Council Social Work Department over capital and revenue funding issues, we decided to proceed.

We were entering entirely new territory for a housing association in Scotland. There were no other examples to go to see; we had to devise an allocation policy specific for this client group and to agree on how much of the building should be funded by a financial contribution from the Health Board's Hospital Closure Programme. Our Committee were naturally a little apprehensive as we seemed to be taking most of the risk. They relied heavily on our two experts on the Committee, Margaret Auld and Donald MacDonald, and the knowledge that Dawn McCraw and some of her team from Dingleton would transferring to our new building on Eildon Employment Contracts.

Two years after those first discussions the building was complete and the patients from Dingleton Hospital duly moved in over a three week period and became residents in their own home. Relatives were encouraged to visit whenever they liked and the three linked houses began to take on their own identity. There was a specially designed garden, incorporating a ha-ha to give residents a view of the surrounding community without the need for a security fence having to be installed to prevent residents wandering outside without a member of staff.

Craw Wood – as the development was called – was a landmark in the design of accommodation for people with dementia and soon after its official opening by John Ward, Chairman of Scottish Homes, we were inundated with requests for visits which we had to ration strictly, in order to protect our residents' privacy.

As can be seen from these examples, a Regional Housing Association operating in a rural area will face a broad range of housing and care challenges. To be successful in delivering such a varied programme requires a Committee with strong leadership and a broad range of skills. Eildon were fortunate in having Bill Wilkie as Chairman throughout these formative years and a stable group of Committee Members with a wide background of skills and knowledge of the Borders.

Nothing, however could have prepared us for what was to happen next.

Stock Transfer

The Scottish Borders Council is one of the few Councils in Scotland that has no council housing. The story of how it ended up with no council housing is a long one with twists and turns that start with the decision of the Government that Scottish Special Housing Association (SSHA) to dispose of its houses in the Borders, all of which were managed by the local authorities for the SSHA.

The SSHA, with the support of the Scottish Office, had intended to transfer all its Borders stock to a completely new organisation to be called Waverley Housing Trust based in Hawick. The Borders was regarded by the Scottish Office as a good place to try out this idea. The process to be successful would require tenant support and private finance. The new organisation was to be headed up by Robert Johnson, the Director of Housing for Roxburgh District Council who was a well-known and well respected figure and this was no doubt seen as a further advantage to guaranteeing the success of this important new housing policy initiative.

If successful, this model could transform the social housing sector in Scotland, bringing much needed private finance to modernise SSHA and Council housing stock and at the same time to relieve Councils of servicing long term loans on the stock. Waverley Housing Trust clearly had the highest political backing, but the way the announcement and launch was not well handled. None of the local authorities affected had been involved in the discussions. Nor had Eildon as the recognised Regional Housing Association serving the Borders. Following a number of meetings, it was agreed that we would be allowed to manage the 180 houses in Tweeddale. With Waverley managing the remaining 1,300. After threes of managing the stock, we would then be allowed to bid for the stock which would be subject to a Tenants' Ballot.

Over the next three years both Eildon and Waverley concentrated on delivering the best service they could for the former SSHA tenants. We opened a new local office in Peebles to demonstrate our commitment to our new tenants in Peebles, Innerleithen and Walkerburn. During this period we were conscious of the need to start preparing our bid to buy the houses and started to survey the properties and build up a picture of the extent of the modernisation programme we would need to promise the tenants in order to win their confidence and eventually their vote.

We also had to understand how the financial modelling worked for this type of acquisition. There was virtually no experience in Scotland about how to raise private finance to fund a stock transfer. We found ourselves on a steep learning curve, to ensure we understood how Business Plan were prepared and the level of detail required about the stock to be purchased that the banks would require before agreeing to a loan. Fortunately on our Committee we had sufficient financial expertise to grasp the basic concepts needed to understand the risks to which we were subjecting the Association. Several trips to London were made to hold meetings with the leading financial consultants who could offer their services based on their experience with large English Housing Associations who had successfully acquired stock in this way.

It soon became clear that the key to making a good bid was to have a sound knowledge of the stock to be purchased and one could not rely on the existing landlord to provide accurate information in sufficient detail. This was relatively easy for the SSHA stock we were managing in Tweeddale, but virtually impossible for the remaining SSHA stock managed by Waverley.

The other key issue was the offer price and how that was arrived at through the Business Plan spreadsheets. We saw ourselves as guinea pigs and some of the basic concepts of how to arrive at a fair price for the stock were evolving. The Scottish Office, who had to approve each transfer, relied heavily on the value placed on the stock by the District Valuer. We and the private lenders wanted to purchase the stock at a price that enabled the backlog of repairs and modernisation programme to be funded within a rent structure that would be acceptable to tenants.

We soon learnt how financial spreadsheets were the device used to manipulate the bid price

To get a higher price you could move some of the high expenditure maintenance items into years thirty-one and beyond, which would give a more favourable bottom line at year thirty when the loan was repaid.

This was difficult for Committee Members to accept and was unlike anything they had done before. Up to that time Eldon's financial position was sound, based on the high levels of Housing Association Grant available at that time. The world of stock transfer finance looked a whole lot more risky, particularly as we were the first Housing Association involved in it.

To the great credit of our Committee, they soon became familiar with this new way of acquiring houses and we found ourselves bidding for the SSHA stock in the Borders. We found ourselves however at a serious disadvantage to Waverley, as we felt we were given insufficient information on the stock they were managing in order to make a competitive bid. Despite us making a protest about the whole manner in which the bidding process was handled, we were successful in making a bid for the Tweeddale SSHA stock we had been managing for three years and Waverley were successful in securing their stock.

Due to the controversy this first attempt at Stock Transfer in Scotland had created, Parliament commissioned the National Audit Office to prepare a report on the whole process, to establish if value for money had been achieved and what lessons could be learnt for future bids.

We cooperated fully in providing information to the investigators and when the report was finally published it concluded that value for money had been obtained in the final bids made by Waverley and Eildon, with some mild criticism of the way information had been released to potential bidders. The overall message from the report was that this first stock transfer was a valuable exercise that proved that the process was sound and that private lenders were willing to fund this type of transaction. Any criticisms identified would be acted on through improving procedures in future stock transfers. This was not entirely our view of the process, but we needed to move on and satisfied ourselves in the knowledge that our experience had helped to improve the way future stock transfers would be handled.

As this was the first successful stock transfer in Scotland to an existing housing association, entirely funded by private finance, we found ourselves in demand by other housing associations wanting to explore   how it was done. We helped a number of rural housing associations to understand the process on an informal basis and prepared bids on an agency basis for Clydesdale and East Lothian Housing Associations. The obvious attraction for rural housing associations with modest development programmes was the ability to become larger overnight and obtain the advantages that are supposed to come with scale. The challenges facing an Association dominated by large unattractive housing estates require a range of new skills that Committee Members may not immediately appreciate. The lure of stock transfer can be a challenge too far for many Committee Members and I often found myself having to stress to those seeking Eildon's advice not to underestimate the strain on limited resources that preparing a bid will create and the unglamorous side of negotiating with Independent Tenant Advisors, reading the fine print of Transfer Agreements and Private Finance negotiations. Stock Transfer is not a panacea for all rural housing associations and needs very careful consideration before embarking on it, not least because your existing tenants may not be too enthusiastic themselves.

In 1996, all-purpose single tier authorities would replace the somewhat cumbersome two tier system of District and Regional Councils that prevailed in Scotland. For the Borders this meant replacing four District Councils, each with their own housing department, and one Regional Council responsible for Planning and Social Work, with an all-purpose authority to be called Scottish Borders Council. This obvious rationalisation was not universally welcomed, particularly in the more rural parts of Tweeddale and Berwickshire which feared a loss of control as power – as they saw it – would concentrate in the two central Districts dominated by the two largest towns of Galashiels and Hawick.

This fear of loss of control was most evident in Berwickshire, where the District Council based in Duns decided to take matters into their own hands in the short time they had between the announcement of the proposed new single tier authority boundaries being made and the date they were to come into operation. To the surprise of everyone, a small group of prominent councillors on Berwickshire District Council decided the best way of preventing their Council Houses being transferred to the new authority based in Newtown St Boswells was to transfer its entire stock into a Housing Association to be created for that purpose. Surprisingly enough, the Scottish Office were willing to support this somewhat radical move, despite opposition from the other District Councils who regarded it as a vote of no confidence in the new Regional Council that was to be formed.

Once again, therefore, the Borders saw itself at the centre of controversy over its social housing stock. After being the first part of Scotland to see the Stock Transfer of former SSHA houses, we were to be the first part of Scotland to see a local authority transfer its entire stock of Council Houses to a new housing association specifically set up for the task. Ironically enough, despite being approached by a number of rural housing associations to advise them on stock transfer possibilities, no one from Berwickshire District Council sought our advice.

The Berwickshire Councillors clearly thought it preferable to retain control of their Council Stock by creating a housing association rather than the stock being transferred to the new single tier authority with its headquarters located twenty-five miles from Duns. They clearly had support from officials in the Scottish Office and, in the short time available, achieved their objective: Berwickshire Housing Association was duly created. We immediately approached the new organisation, as we had housing stock and a rolling development programme in their area. George Finlay, their first Chairman, and Philip Jones, their new Director, assured us they had no plans for development and their first task was to improve the stock of the 1,800 Council Houses they inherited.

We were at first reassured that Berwickshire would leave the development of new HAG funded houses to us and we would cooperate with them as they concentrated on setting up the organisation. As time went by, Berwickshire began to be interested in developing new houses and had a number of sites they had acquired as part of the Stock Transfer deal. Initially it was agreed we would act as their development agents, but they soon made it clear they had their own ideas and philosophy for development and we decided to leave them to it. We continued over the years to cooperate on a number of issues and meet on a regular basis through the Borders Housing Forum set up by the new Council to discuss common housing issues.

As soon as Scottish Borders Council was formed, their first task was to manage the 8,000 Council Houses they had inherited from Tweeddale, Roxburgh and Ettrick and Lauderdale District Councils and rationalise allocation, maintenance and rent policies. The new Housing Department was led by Hamish Blacklaws, the former Director of Housing for Ettrick and Lauderdale District Council, and Janice Cambridge, former Head of Housing at Tweeddale District Council. They were both strong supporters of Eildon and both had helped us to identify sites; we were keen to carry on our relationship with them and their new councillors to continue our role to bring the maximum investment through the HAG Programme for more new houses that was so desperately needed.

It soon became clear that the new Local Authority had insufficient resources to match the funding that Waverley, Berwickshire and ourselves had available to make the necessary investment required to modernise their stock. As time went by, their stock would decline in quality as the stock of

Waverley and Berwickshire would gradually improve through the guaranteed modernisation programmes promised to their tenants at transfer. Eildon had also modernised all its SSHA stock in Tweeddale following transfer and all the remaining stock was of a high standard, having been built over the previous ten years.

Without significantly increasing rents, which would have been politically unacceptable, it was difficult to see how the council's 8,000 houses could be modernised. The only option remaining seemed to be to go down the Stock Transfer route and for Scottish Borders Council to form their own housing association as Berwickshire District Council had done. Given the somewhat unfortunate way the two previous stock transfers had gone in the Borders, there was no immediate enthusiasm for this idea from Councillors. Both Janice Cambridge and later Hamish Blacklaws could see the need to explore ways to modernise their stock without dramatically increasing rents. Informal meetings took place at staff level to see how this might be achieved, which resulted in a bid being made to the Scottish Office for funding to explore with consultants what options could be pursued,

Clearly some form of Stock Transfer to either existing or new housing associations was the option to be explored. Given the opportunistic way the two previous stock transfers had happened, there was an opportunity to look at rationalising the number of social landlords in the Borders as part of any further stock transfer process.

When I came to the Borders in 1985 there were four Housing Authorities, managing 13,000 houses.

If Scottish Borders Council were to transfer their stock to a new housing association, we would end up with four regulated social landlords instead. The question was, does the Borders with its population of 105,000 people need four housing associations and would fewer organisations offer greater efficiencies that would benefit tenants? Both Eildon and Berwickshire Housing Associations agreed to work together to explore with Scottish Borders Council possible options for rationalising the way a stock transfer of the remaining stock could take place. Scottish Borders Council were successful in their application for funding to appoint consultants to bring forward possible options and HACAS, well-respected private consultants in the field of Stock Transfer, were duly appointed.

This was a significant and potentially exciting move by the three parties concerned and a credit to Committee Members and Councillors who were willing to look objectively at what would be best for tenants in the Borders as a whole and not merely what was best for each existing organisation.

The overriding objective for Scottish Borders Council was to bring forward proposals that would eliminate the Council's Housing debt and attract up to £60 million of private investment to spend on bringing the Council's stock up to an acceptable standard. HACAS were also to consider what advantages there might be if Eildon and Berwickshire HA's stock was to be included to create a single organisation of approximately 11,300 houses, resulting in one of the largest housing associations in Scotland. A number of alternative structures were considered, based on Group Structures which were common in England for the large housing associations operating there.

The final option that it was agreed would be presented to tenants was a merger of Eildon and Scottish Borders Council stock into a new organisation to be called Scottish Borders Housing Association. This was a big decision for Eildon, as in effect we would be working for our own demise if the process was to succeed. In the many years I have worked in the housing association sector I have repeatedly come across Committees who wanted at all costs to retain their identity. The way housing associations have developed in rural areas is often the result of accident rather than design. An association may be formed initially by a dedicated group of people who want to resolve a specific problem or by a group of professionals who want to take advantage of a new policy initiative. These associations may thrive and grow or simply stagnate after fulfilling a particular need. As a method of distributing national resources related to housing need, the network of local organisations in rural Scotland is far from rational. What we do have, however, is a great variety of housing organisations, with some extraordinary individuals giving many hours of their time to help those in need.

In 2000 therefore it was agreed to work with HACAS who would act as impartial consultants to support a Shadow Board consisting of Members from Eildon's Board and Scottish Borders Council, supported by senior staff from the Council's Housing Department and Eldon's Management Team. Representatives from Eildon's Tenants Organisation and the Council's Tenants Group were also invited onto the Shadow Board.

Despite working well together at Shadow Board level, the ambitious proposals to merge Eildon and the Council's housing stock into one operation proved too complex to deliver, particularly when trying to explain to tenants what the advantage to them would be. Eildon tenants were already well housed, either living in new housing developments recently completed or in ex SSHA stock which had been modernised. For Eildon tenants it all began to look too risky and it was with reluctance that we agreed to shelve the idea of a merger until a later date.

Despite this decision, Eildon's Board decided to offer every assistance to the Shadow Board of SBHA and Eildon's Chairman Bill Wilkie and Vice Chair Margaret Auld agreed to continue to sit on the Shadow Board with myself and Laurence Cox, our Development Director, being seconded two days a week to help Janice Cambridge and her team to prepare the Business Plan.

In November 2001 a successful tenants' ballot was held with the transfer of the 8,000 houses to the new housing association to be known as SBHA-Scottish Borders Housing Association taking place in the summer of 2002. Soon after Eildon entered into an Agency Agreement with SBHA to provide the technical services they required to deliver their modernisation programme. Bill Wilkie and Margaret Auld continued to sit on their Board to give support to their new Chairman Oliver Angus.

So it was that by 2002, just twelve years after Waverley Housing surprised us all, all the social housing in the Borders had been transferred into four not for profit housing associations or trusts.

Working together

Despite the turbulent events of the past thirty years, much cooperation exists between the four housing organisations and Scottish Borders Council. Regular meetings have always been held through the Borders Housing Forum, which has resulted in many new initiatives for the benefit of everyone who lives here.

The following services are just a few examples demonstrating this level of cooperation and joint working:

Border Choice Homes – Berwickshire, Waverley and Eildon operate a choice-based common housing register. Each week all the vacant properties of each landlord are advertised in the local press and on-line, allowing those in housing need to bid for the properties of their choice.

Borders Care and Repair Service – this service is provided by Eildon Enterprise, a subsidiary of Eildon Housing Association delivering a programme of Wider Action services. This is a partnership with Scottish Borders Council and provides a Home Improvement Service, a Handy-persons Service and an Adaptations Service. The aim of all these services is to enable older people and those with a physical disability to remain in their homes and feel safe and there. Started in 2005, this range of services has proved extremely popular and helps thousands of owner occupiers and tenants to feel secure in their homes.

Borders Construction Industry Forum (BCIF) – this was formed in 2002, following a successful bid for European Funding. Eildon supported by Communities Scotland, Scottish Enterprise Borders and Scottish Borders Council became a key sponsor of the Forum, providing them with office accommodation and administrative services. The main aim of the Forum is to provide local construction companies based in the Borders with information and training they require to be able to compete successfully for contracts in the increasingly complex tendering procedures required by public sector clients.

In addition to organising seminars and visits for BCIF Members, Eildon also provides testing facilities for Health and Safety Certificates required by Building Operatives before they can work on site. In this way Eildon helps those small to medium sized building contractors in the Borders who have historically built the majority of housing developments here.

Challenges and opportunities ahead

Despite the tremendous changes experienced in the Borders over the past thirty years in the field of social housing, there are still significant challenges to be addressed. There is still a shortage of affordable housing and, as the population ages, we will need to adapt our housing provision to cope with demand.

Nile Istephan, who joined Eildon in 2010 as its Chief Executive gives his assessment of what still needs to be done:

Borders Housing Associations are now well established organisations within the local political and economic landscape, and are increasingly recognised as a driving force for innovation. Housing need across our rural communities remains a key focus, and the delivery of new homes to meet this need continues to be a major achievement. Whilst grant support is more restricted and the lending environment is more challenging than in the past, affordable housing development is now being used to unlock private housing developments, which can be seen most clearly with the Borders biggest land release at Easter Langlee in Galashiels being opened up following significant affordable housing investment. Although house completions in the Borders have dipped considerably in recent years, the affordable housing programme has provided a consistent new supply of homes, both meeting needs and supporting jobs in the hard pressed construction industry. Borders Associations also continue to innovate in the provision of new homes, with increasingly high standards, new construction methods and tenures such as Mid-Market Rented Homes.

As well as meeting demand from new supply, Housing Associations in the Borders have been investing heavily in existing stock through modernisation programmes. This investment has supported a range of projects aimed at addressing the significant issue of fuel poverty, which is more prevalent in rural communities. Sustainable technologies are being creatively used in all communities and these are now effectively mainstreamed in the Borders affordable housing stock. With increasing fuel costs, a challenging economic environment and a significant element of the area not connected to the gas network, addressing fuel poverty issues remains a key focus.

The four main Borders Housing Associations are an integral part of the community planning structures within the Borders and are leading strands of partnership activity around anti-poverty measures, delivering a low carbon economy and reforming the delivery of public services. As community anchor organisations each of the Associations is fully connected with the various communities where they have presence and are coordinating efforts to engage with local groups and address the needs of the local population. Borders Associations continue to deliver valuable 'wider role' services such as highly successful employability programmes, and the nationally recognised integrated Care & Repair service. There is strong track record of partnership working with the statuary agencies and also collaboration, co-operation and sharing of services and expertise amongst the Housing Associations, and this continues to grow and develop.

This is most recently evident in collective efforts to help ensure housing issues are fully recognised within the emerging health and social care integration process.

Borders Housing Associations have grown to be much more than simply landlords renting out homes to tenants, and they are set to continue to develop further in the period ahead based on being innovative, responsive, well governed organisations rooted in the communities they know and understand."

PART THREE

Where next?

2015
Rural Housing associations today and tomorrow

It is now twenty-five years since the Scottish Homes Rural Policy was launched. Much has changed since then. Few could have predicted the changes that have come about – a different local Government structure, a Scottish Parliament, and the financial crash are just some of the big national changes that have had an impact on how that policy could be delivered. In the world of housing associations, there have also been huge changes. Even the name has changed to Registered Social Landlord (RSL). The share of housing provision that the sector (or can it still called a movement?) owns has dramatically increased thanks to stock transfer (although the impact of Right to Buy cannot be underestimated). The RSL world has become much more complex. Regulation has changed significantly with the Regulator focusing on the interests of tenants, homeless persons and other users. The old HAG regime has gone; the financing of capital projects now involves much more complex funding arrangements. And the way the Scottish Government plans, supports and oversees the sector have completely changed. Not only has Scottish Homes disappeared, but also its successor Communities Scotland with the role being undertaken by the Government itself. And Scottish Homes is now looked upon with fond memory!

Although the phrase 'rural housing' is still used, it is appearing less and less in official documentation. The current Government's housing strategy *'Homes Fit for the 21st Century'* does not have a separate rural section. It is difficult these days to try to analyse rural housing investment below local authority area. There may be a national rural definition (communities under 3,000), but there is no publicly available analysis of how far housing investment is being made in accessible or remote communities across Scotland. Which means that we are back to where Scotland's latest three cities – Inverness, Stirling and Perth – may continue to dominate the housing provision in their local authority areas. And as for Arran . . .

The housing options that are now available to individual households are much greater than available in 1990 – particularly the range of 'low cost' homeownership (LCHO) options designed to give households a leg up onto the first rung of the homeownership ladder. While Right to Buy is now being brought to an end by the Scottish Government, the supply of new, additional and genuinely affordable rented housing opportunities will always be limited by the degree of annual public investment. However the overall stock of rented Council and housing association will, henceforth, grow steadily bigger. At a national level, Shared Equity schemes such as Open Market Shared Equity, New Supply Shared Equity Scheme, New Supply Shared Equity Scheme with Developers, MI New Home, Help to Buy (Scotland) are just some of the LCHO mechanisms that have been developed to boost affordable homeownership. These sit alongside developments such as the National Housing Trust. And, in some areas – particularly in the Highlands – schemes pioneered by The Highlands Small Communities Housing Trust are adding to the opportunities.

There is no doubt that, in a time of highly restricted public finance, governments try to stretch the available resources, and low cost home ownership initiatives help to achieve that objective. And in rural areas, the demand for home ownership remains very high. As Di Alexander explains *LCHO options deliver a number of policy benefits, including a reduction in the cost to the public purse of helping a significant proportion of the people in affordable housing need to both resolve their housing problem and achieve their aspiration of building their own homes or getting them built for them when the alternative solution, of building a new Council or Housing Association house for rent, costs between two to three times as much public money per unit. So supporting affordable homeownership in this way makes both the public and the private money invested work harder and deliver more housing opportunities for a greater number of people and communities. It helps to target public investment more efficiently and beneficially on rural and remote economies knowing that one-off new build contracts are most likely to go to local builders who employ local people. It helps free up some Council and Housing Association houses as tenants are assisted to achieve their affordable homeownership aspirations. And, provided the Rural Housing Burden legal mechanism is applied to the LCHO transaction, then it secures the affordability benefits of the public money invested in perpetuity and delivers a slow but steady accretion of a permanently affordable housing component to the particular community's homeownership market which otherwise financially excludes the great majority of ordinary rural households who may aspire to join it.*

And who are the people most likely to want to invest long term in building and owning and living in their own homes in Scotland's many and varied rural and remote communities? Their lifeblood, their prime assets: those newly formed and forming families, the younger, socially and economically active adults whose children fill the local school and keep the pulse of the community beating strongly'.

But even without statistics to prove it, from the work done by housing associations, and the research undertaken by organisations like Rural Housing Scotland, it is clear that much has been achieved over the last twenty five years. Housing associations have risen to the challenge of meeting rural housing needs in their own distinctive way. They have grasped opportunities as they became available, often against odds that would have put off less committed bodies. And because so many have very local roots, the determination of the staff and – even more – the voluntary committee members have seen homes delivered in small projects in communities which have able to survive and thrive by retaining and building up a local population. Older people have been kept in their own home through Care and Repair or in their own community with purpose built housing with both social and economic advantages. Younger people have been able to stay and create businesses or remain in jobs and bring up a family in the places they want to be, with the result that schools remain open – a key lifeline for the future of rural sustainable communities. Energy advice has been offered to many households. Housing associations have become anchor organisations in many communities. In larger Council areas (like Highland) a local association delivers additional flexibility for the local authority and provides an ability to be closer to the customer.

The continuing challenge

But much remains to be done. While the published housing statistics may not be available on the basis of SGURC (Scottish Government Urban Rural Classification), it is possible to get a clearer picture by looking at what public information is available through the *Scottish House Conditions Survey* (SHCS), the Scottish Government's publication *Rural Scotland Key Facts 2015*, the Rural Policy Centre's *Rural Scotland in Focus 2014,* along with the work done by academics and others.

The **SHCS** now records quality on a continuous basis. It records changes over time and looks at the physical condition of Scotland's homes as well as the experience of householders. One of the key areas it records is progress against the current minimum standard, the Scottish Housing Quality Standard. For 2013, SHCS shows that while there has been a considerable improvement, much remains to be done. Using the last four years of published information, only 31% of houses in rural Scotland met the Quality Standard in 2010. By 2013 this had risen to 45%; however this still lags behind urban at 52% (SHCS has only one category of rural – communities less than 3,000 population). Disrepair is however, slightly better in rural areas.

In recording that the quality of the existing stock has improved, neither the Scottish Housing Quality Standard nor the Scottish House Conditions Survey looks at the quality of the building design. Since the Richards' 1994 report, much has changed and the outlook is good. Housing design in rural Scotland has improved. Rural Scotland has attracted architects to move in or stay, and some of the best architecture is now being produced at reasonable cost. Architectural innovation is also a feature, and housing associations have played their part as progressive clients, and have become leaders in housing innovation and design, with particular emphasis on energy and sustainability. As the stories from the individual associations have shown, association homes regularly feature in the various housing awards – including Saltire Housing Awards and Scottish Home Awards.

The *Key Facts* document throws up other issues.

Fuel poverty is one which rural and island associations are significantly tackling though they are determined to do more. Groups like Highlands and Islands Housing Associations Affordable Warmth Working Group (with the wonderful nickname of Heehaw) have been lobbying for equitable pricing for rural customers and developing a proposal for an Energycare project, based on the successful Care & Repair approach, to tackle the issues of hard-to-heat and hard-to-treat problems affecting so many older homes and households.

The chart opposite demonstrates the seriousness of fuel poverty in rural Scotland, compared to the rest of Scotland

A recent study for Comhairle nan Eilean Siar showed that 71% of households in the Western Isles spend more than 10% of their income on fuel. This is the highest level of fuel poverty, not just in Scotland, but in the whole of the UK.

Fuel poverty in rural Scotland, compared to the rest of Scotland.

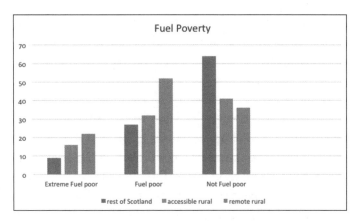

The population age profile also highlights concerns that impact on the provision of housing. The child population (up to sixteen) is relatively similar to the rest of Scotland. Between sixteen and twenty-four and between twenty-five and thirty-four it is significantly less similar. The percentage of the population between twenty-five and thirty-four in remote rural is 9% compared to 14% in the rest of Scotland. At the other end of the age range, remote rural has 23% over 65s compared to 17% in the rest of Scotland. In some cases, the proportion of over 65's is even higher; in many remoter settlements of the Highlands and Islands the proportion can be over a third and more. The case for Care and Repair continuing would appear to clear; however, access to housing for younger households may well still be a major key to sustainable rural communities. In a recent survey for HIE, 93% of young people believe good access to housing is critical for attracting them to live, work and study in the Highlands and Islands. And there is no reason to doubt that similar results would come from the rest of Scotland. The report by ekosgen states 'Access *to housing is a big barrier for young people: almost half of all young people live in the parental home (up till age 30); almost twice the proportion nationally for those aged 20–35 years. Access to housing to buy, or even rent, is regarded as limited, with this being particularly acute in the Outer Hebrides and Shetland. Whilst market conditions and access to credit/mortgages challenges are not unique to the Highlands and Islands, the lack of available and affordable housing is a particular barrier'.*

Social rent provision at 14% (2013 figures) compares perhaps unfavourably against 25% for the rest of Scotland. And despite appearances and history, there is more private rented accommodation in the rest of

Scotland at 14% compared to rural at 11%. The main rural tenure is still owner-occupation. But house prices are known to be higher than the rest of Scotland (with average accessible rural house prices being around 50% above those in the rest of Scotland). Accessing home ownership remains difficult for those on lower incomes and those starting on the housing ladder (who may be the one and the same). They may also be competing against retirees who are downsizing. To find a house means accessing social rented accommodation or some way of getting on the housing ladder, and there is less social rented housing.

Rural Scotland in Focus looks to the future. Population projections suggest that between 2010 and 2035 the housing stock will need to increase by 20% with large regional variations – e.g. Aberdeenshire at 32% compared with Eilean Siar at 8%, Dumfries and Galloway at 4% and Argyll and Bute at 1%. Because the figures are calculated on a Council area basis, the likelihood is that most of the growth is likely to be in accessible rural areas. Looking at settlements, the report highlights that of the 208 settlements with a population of under 3,000 in 2001, 18% had grown by more than a quarter by 2011. The majority of these were within easy commuting distance of large towns and cities. On the other hand, small settlements (≥1,000) or medium size (1,000 to 2,000) were the ones most likely to lose population. The report is not able, of course, to identify whether any of this is due to development planning. In the case of RSLs, it cannot say whether the funding and planning regimes have created a presumption against development in smaller communities. The impact of the recession on rural RSLs house building programme appears to have lagged behind that of the private sector, where reductions in completions took place from 2008, although RSL completions rapidly reduced from 2010 onwards. This was as a consequence of significant reductions in grant levels combined with restrictive and onerous conditions introduced by High Street lenders; as a result many rural associations had either to severely curtail their development programmes or stop building new houses altogether, although recently improved grant funding and lending conditions have improved the position.

2015
Into the future

This book took as a starting point the Rural Forum report of 1984. The report had three concerns:

- The poor physical condition of the housing stock
- The lack of accommodation for those on lower incomes
- The financial cutbacks that had reduced new construction

In the thirty years since then, after much innovation and investment, the position, though improved, sounds not dissimilar:

- The poor energy efficiency of the housing stock
- The lack of sufficient affordable accommodation for those on lower (and in some cases middle) incomes
- The financial challenges that inhibit small scale new construction

Energy efficiency

Energy efficiency, and the issue of affordable warmth, is now being dealt with as a cornerstone of the National Infrastructure Priority and as part of the Climate Change Action programme. This backs up commitments already made to tackling fuel poverty through housing programmes. The question for rural housing is how far the programmes will be 'rural proofed' to recognise the additional energy charges and the amount of 'off gas' housing in more remote Scotland. The experience of associations in providing Care and Repair and Handyman services, in providing energy advice, and in renewable energy, should stand them in good stead to make a major contribution to this Government programme which will also bring in additional resources. Most recently, the Government has established the Scottish Rural Fuel Poverty Task Force under the chairmanship of Di Alexander and including a number of housing association people to propose practical solutions to the challenges in rural areas.

Supply and finance

Dealing with the lack of affordable housing can only mean one thing – supply must be increased. There remain some opportunities to increase access to existing houses through the Scottish Empty Homes Partnership run by Shelter working closely with local authorities' Empty Homes Officers. Bringing private rented vacant stock back into use cannot solve the supply issue alone, but it makes vital contribution.

Increasing supply through new building is essential as rural Scotland continues to attract people to continue living or to come and live in the countryside. Housing associations, as local anchor organisations, are well placed to deliver new homes in partnership with local authorities, economic agencies and other voluntary bodies and social enterprises. And increasing supply also means dealing with the financial challenges. They are interlinked.

RSLs are of course not alone. In the Highlands and in Dumfries & Galloway community housing trusts have been developed to deliver additional affordable housing opportunities where needed. A number of local authorities themselves have begun to build new houses again. Significantly, some community groups are trying out new approaches to provide affordable housing to rent – effectively becoming a community landlord. Ulva School Community Association in Mull is one of the pioneers, with support from Mull and Iona Community Trust who are employing a housing manager and will take on the long term responsibilities of owning and renting the two houses. Funding is coming from the Community Land Fund, Argyll & Bute Council, and from local fundraising. It will be interesting to see if and how 'crowdfunding' works for rural housing.

These early examples of communities wanting to provide housing without becoming an RSL themselves may be the beginnings of the model of the English Community Land Trusts (CLT). In CLTs, communities draw on the local housing association's or regional housing trust's housing development and financial management know-how to help them reduce the pain and difficulty of actually building the affordable houses they want to have but without usurping the community's right, through its CLT, to retain the ownership and ultimate control over the land the houses are built on. And, as a consequence, the ownership, use and destiny of the houses themselves and the ordinary members of the community whose needs they exist to serve.

Proposes houses at Ulva Ferry.
Drawing copyright Thorne Wyness Architects.

Alongside this, existing landowners like Andrew Bradford of Kincardine O'Neil in Deeside have been adding to their rented portfolio for some time and will continue do so, often at comparative rents and housing people who are on local authority housing lists. They of course do not have to take land cost into account. Which is one of the issues that still limits housing associations in their development programmes. New mechanisms like The National Housing Trust may be available and may help in mid-rent schemes, but if we are to prevent rural Scotland outside the bigger towns becoming gentrified, more may still need to be done. The key challenges of land, planning development, costs, social housing provision and rural proofing still remain.

Land

Land remains a key challenge. Without land, there can be no new homes. Di Alexander's maxim *'first the land, then the houses'* remains at the heart of the rural housing challenge, but the land must be *affordable* to deliver *affordable* housing. Over the years attempts have been made to find ways of accessing land by negotiation, by persuasion, and by using the planning system. Land reform and community asset ownership are important contributions to the future. Some mechanisms have been developed and should be used more widely, like Rural Housing Burdens. Models such as The Highlands Small Communities Housing Trust, and the Highland Housing Alliance could be repeated across the country, as the Rural Affairs and Environment Committee noted. But are they enough? In their 2014 report the Land Reform Review Group proposed the establishment of a Land and Property Commission to help *'make Scotland's system of land-ownership a more efficient and effective system for delivering the public interest'.* The OECD suggested that more direct action was needed, as did the Rural Affairs and Environment Committee and as Scottish Homes considered in 1998. This might mean Compulsory Purchase (CPO). If the provision of affordable housing is essential for the future of the economic development of rural Scotland, then should housing, or at the least the provision of land for housing, be treated more as part of infrastructure? CPOs are regarded as a normal part of road building and other infrastructure. Why not housing?

Planning

Planning can still be a challenge. Despite the attempts of the Rural Affairs Committee and the development of Affordable Housing Policies, there remains a cultural attitude towards small scale affordable housing whether social rent or low cost home ownership, and not just within the planning professions. It is effectively a presumption against development. It is sometimes seen as a 'NIMBY' problem, where any further development is unwelcome, even more so where the development is for people on lower incomes. It is sometimes seen as a 'sustainability' problem, where sustainable communities are considered only possible in larger communities, and where public transport can provide mobility for people on lower incomes. It is sometimes seen as 'environmental protection' problem, designed to protect the countryside from creeping development. All of this is a reinforcement of the 'townie' view of rural Scotland as a good place to visit and as a place where change should be discouraged. Or if it has to change then only big expensive houses are acceptable, and these, often in converted steadings, could be seen as the rural equivalent of 'gated communities'. Is gentrification what is wanted?

Development costs

Balancing the costs of development is a challenge. Land, transport of materials, grid connection charges, meeting new housing and building regulation standards all add to the costs. And these costs are generally higher in rural Scotland, and in particular in smaller developments in island and more remote parts of the country. The pressure to reduce costs once more creates the push to locate affordable housing in the bigger centres. But local solutions or 'hand crafted pies' are still what smaller communities need to be sustainable communities. Anything that is hand crafted may cost more than mass production. But rural communities have become adept at achieving value for money; new housing designed for local circumstances, using locally sourced materials and built by local contractors can have a local economic impact as well as provide new accommodation. That holistic view of investment, of supporting the sustainability of rural communities should be at the heart of public funded investment decisions.

In looking at the mechanisms for supporting low cost home ownership (LCHO) in more remote communities there is a case for reviving the Rural Home Ownership Grant (RHOG). Di Alexander points out that *'if a "comeback RHOG" met 15% of the overall development cost (or roughly the same average grant levels as crofters get to build their new homes) then by adding this discount to the one given on the land sale price of, say, 25%, Government could ensure that around 40% of the equity would be retained in perpetuity as the combined affordability discount to defray the market price. Thus a home which on the open market would cost £150,000 could be bought for 40% less, bringing it even further within the affordability range of a much larger section of the local housing market.'*

Social renting provision

Increasing the provision of the most affordable form of housing – social rented housing – in Scotland's rural and remoter communities, remains a major challenge. With its typically greater development costs and challenges, its subsequent requirement for higher levels of public investment and with owner-occupation as the dominant tenure and aspiration in rural areas, the temptation is there to simply develop more – and less subsidy hungry – LCHO at the expense of social rented provision. Much of the debate about social rent over the last couple of decades has been about creating mixed communities by introducing home ownership in urban areas dominated by social renting. If mixed communities are to be encouraged in rural Scotland, then that issue has to be turned on its head; social rented housing (along with good quality private rented housing at affordable rent) remains absolutely vital to enable the maintenance and development of socially and economically mixed populations. And the housing associations need to be adequately resourced to provide rented homes which remain properly affordable. Building LCHO housing involves less public money, and can make the output numbers look good, but the outcome may not be what is needed. Scottish Government has previously stated that housing associations should be supported to create a balanced programme of two-thirds social rented housing and one-third LCHO housing but a relative increase in LCHO has been suggested by some commentators even although local housing needs surveys and surgeries not infrequently show that the affordable social rented need may be even greater than 2:1. This is not to argue against low cost home ownership; home ownership remains the ultimate preference for most rural dwellers. But given the ownership pattern in the existing rural housing stock, the impact of Right to Buy (even although it is now ending) and the contribution of house builders – all of which help owner-occupation, the predominant need in many rural communities remains for affordable rented accommodation and public planning and investment priorities must continue to respond responsibly to this reality.

Easterbister Road, Kirkwall.
Photo from Orkney HA

Rural proofing

'Rural proofing' remains the challenge in all of this. The Rural Affairs and Environment Committee recognised this (if they had not, who would?).

Rural housing issues need to be treated as a different challenge to urban housing. While much is the same, the differences are sufficient to warrant different approaches, even a different policy, which is why Scottish Homes developed one. It's partly about scale – small communities need small scale solutions; it's partly about land – land acquisition is a different issue in rural Scotland; it's partly about money – hand crafted pies may be more expensive; it's partly about planning – sustainability has to some degree been hijacked by those who say that only urban communities are sustainable. But it is mainly about culture. It's about the way townies (including those who live in rural towns) regard the countryside. And the need for clear policies that reflect these rural context differences. In addition, there is a case for even better coordination of housing, economic and rural development.

Over the years, housing policy in Scotland has moved from simply being about bricks and mortar, supply and condition. It has become both a key part of the Government's procurement policy and integrated into the regeneration agenda, which, given the nature of that agenda, is primarily urban focused. When the Scottish Homes Rural Policy was being developed, there were questions about whether the team and the funding delivering the policy in the Highlands and Islands should become part of Highlands and Islands Enterprise. Certainly it would have allowed for a properly integrated development strategy for that part of Scotland. A strong case can be made for a Rural Development Agency for Scotland which would work closely with HIE in the Highlands and Islands, but not duplicate HIE's work, and be responsible for rural development in the rest of Scotland. Its remit would include rural housing policy as part of its regeneration strategy. It would certainly be one way of ensuring 'rural proofing'.

Or is there an alternative? In the twenty-five years since the rural policy was launched, we have seen not only rural housing but housing as a whole take a lower profile in Government policy and indeed in priority. The question that faces many for whom housing is the priority is whether a greater housing policy is now required or even the creation of a national housing agency such as Scottish Homes. However, three key things have changed since the last Government housing agency. First, the majority of Scots are now well housed. Long gone are the days when one in four households shared an outside toilet, or when serious overcrowding required a national campaign about provision. There are still pockets –

some of them quite large – of both under provision and below standard quality, but these are usually highlighted in local strategies. Second, again for the majority of Scots, our homes are provided by the private sector – whether owning or renting. Any regulation of that sector is done through planning and building regulations, and through consumer regulations. Third, strategic planning including analysis of demand lies within the responsibilities of local authorities. Skills have been built up there and, operating on the principle of subsidiarity; that is the right place for planning for household growth or decline and where local markets can be best understood. And this encourages housing to be seen in the wider context of local development. The impact of the Rural Housing Development Forums from Highland Council provides a successful model of how well-integrated planning and, crucially, the on-the-ground delivery can be achieved.

There are concerns that, given the emphasis on urban growth (even in local authorities with large rural hinterland) and on sustainability being seen as pro-urban, the needs of small scale affordable rural housing are being forgotten and that some kind of Government rural housing agency could help to create a new version of the 'hand crafted pies' approach to rural housing. But, as has been seen, rural housing is not simply about housing units. It plays a fundamental role in ensuring the sustainability of rural communities, and of preventing rural Scotland becoming gentrified. It has been seen and needs to continue to be seen as an integral and indivisible part of community development and regeneration. And many of these small rural communities – villages and townships – want to play a major role in shaping the future for their community – emulating the example of those island and mainland communities that have bought and now control their island or land. Pioneering communities like Helmsdale, Knoydart, Ulva Ferry and Iona that have struggled to create their own small developments of affordable houses have benefited from the professional support that comes through a rural housing enabler. Other communities, like Gigha, have benefited from the close connection with a local housing association. In all cases, the motivation for new houses comes from the need to ensure the long term sustainability of the community as a thriving place to live and work, with opportunities available to a wide range of people regardless of income since communities need a variety of people to make them work. Which means providing affordable housing as part of development and a way of preventing gentrification.

And finally, what of the associations?

This book has attempted to chart the story of rural based housing associations in Scotland. While the first part of the book concentrated on the policy development, the second part told the story from the perspective of those who have risen to the challenge of making the policy work in rural Scotland.. The thread that runs through this book is that of a commitment to the local community. A commitment that is founded on the principle that *'each and every individual community has a right, if it so chooses to exercise it, to make a carefully considered and locally inclusive decision on what kind of affordable housing it needs and where in their community it would most appropriately be located'* (Di Alexander). And it is because these associations play a wider role in their communities beyond the provision of homes that the book has primarily focused on them. This is not to discount the contribution of associations based outwith rural Scotland or the roles played by local authorities and local housing trusts.

The local rural and island associations themselves have matured. They were created within a relatively short time. With the exception of those established because of stock transfer, no new local rural association has been established since the late 1990s. The heady pioneering days that our voices have recounted are long gone. They have become local institutions in their own right, providing a crucial and integrated part of the overall provision of housing across rural Scotland. While new development does occur (albeit at a much slower rate than in the early days and certainly much less than either their aspiration or capacity), their primary function is as a landlord and care provider.

However, while they may be institutions, they have not become institutionalised. They continue to be innovative, responsive to local communities and to the changing needs in those communities. And to survive they will have to continue to change and adapt. They will need to continue to attract local leadership of the calibre that created them who come with a passion for the sustainable future of their communities. This can be less easy when the principle task is managing existing housing. Development is always more exciting than maintenance. The high level professionalism of staff that is required to ensure a high quality service to tenants and other 'customers', with all the rules and regulations, may not seem as motivating as the informal days in the past. But the marks of maturity are to combine the provision of a high level of service with innovation and ingenuity. And there is evidence that rural associations will be capable of being those kind or organisations.

The heart of each housing association is its voluntary committee members. They give up their spare time; some regularly drive long round trips to attend meetings. They take responsibility for community assets worth millions, and get little public recognition for it. But they are concerned about the housing conditions of the people in their communities and the long term sustainability of these communities. They are the people with local knowledge and the local commitment. In many cases they have taken the road from being a small housing organisation and developed it to become an anchor organisation in their community, providing much more that bricks and mortar – the foundation of a thriving sustainable community. Rural Scotland would be the poorer without them, and many more people would still be living in caravans and other substandard and insupportable housing circumstances.

The rural RSLs/housing associations that have developed over the more than thirty years since the Rural Forum report have responded in different ways to their local challenges. Rural Scotland is not homogenous, although there are similarities. If the Scottish Government's aim to promote development in rural areas and empower communities is to be achieved, affordable housing has to be at the heart of that policy. Rural and island housing associations have demonstrated that they have a natural instinct for the innovation, perseverance and commitment that is needed to continue to play a major role in making that aim a reality. But more importantly, they continue to prove that they support the rural communities they serve to be thriving and sustainable.

Further Reading

A+DS Sust (2011) *Scotland's Housing Expo – Case Study* A+DS Edinburgh

Alexander, D., (2011) *Rural Housing Burdens – How effective have they been?* Carnegie UK

Alexander, D., Shucksmith, M., Lindsay, N., (1988) *Scotland's Rural Housing – Opportunities for Action,* Shelter & Rural Forum

Barke, J., (1950) *Land of the Leal* Canongate, Edinburgh

Begg, T. (1996) *Housing Policy in Scotland* John Donald Publishers, Edinburgh

Corbett, G., & Logie, D. (1997) Scotland's Rural Housing: At the Heart of Communities, Shelter & Rural Forum

ekosgen (2015) *Our Next Generation* HIE

HIDB (1974) *House Improvement Surveys Barra 1972* Special Report 12. HIDB

Highlands and Islands Enterprise (2013) *A Minimum Income Standard for Remote Rural Scotland* HIE

Hunter, J., (2012) *From the Low Tide of the Sea to the Highest Mountain Tops – community ownership of land in the Highlands and Islands of Scotland,* Carnegie UK/Islands Book Trust

Land Reform Review Group Final Report (2014) *The Land of Scotland and the Common Good* Scottish Government, Edinburgh

MacGregor, B. D., Robertson, D.S., Shucksmith, M. (1988) *Rural Housing in Scotland* Aberdeen University Press

OECD (2009) *Rural Policy Reviews – Scotland, UK* OECD

Richards, J., & M. (1994) *Timber Frame Housing in the Scottish Countryside* HMSO

Rural Affairs and Environment Committee (2009) *5th Report, 2009 (Session 3) Rural Housing* Scottish Parliament

Rural Policy Centre (2014) *Rural Scotland in Focus* SAC

Satsangi, M., Gallent, N., & Bevan, M. (2010) *The Rural Housing Question* The Policy Press

Sim, D., (ed.), (2004) *Housing and Public Policy in post-devolution in Scotland* CIH

Scottish Executive (2000) *Rural Scotland: a new approach*, The Stationery Office

SFHA (2015) *40 Years of Housing Scotland* Scottish Federation of Housing Associations. Glasgow

Scottish Homes (1990) *The Rural Housing Challenge*, Scottish Homes, Edinburgh

Scottish Homes (1990) *Rural Policy*, Scottish Homes, Edinburgh

Scottish Homes (1998) *Tackling Rural Housing*, Scottish Homes, Edinburgh

Shucksmith, M. (1984) *Scotland's Rural Housing – A Forgotten Problem* Rural Forum

The Energy Advisory Service (2014) *Fuel Poverty Report 2014* TEAS/Comhairle nan Eilean Siar

Young, R.K. (2013) *Annie's Loo* Argyll